CHRIST JESUS DULY PRIZED

AN EXPOSITION ON PHILIPPIANS III. 8-9

Thomas Boston

Vintage Puritan
GLH Publishing
LOUISVILLE, KY

Sourced from *The Whole Works of the Late Reverend Thomas Boston*, Vol. III.
Edited by Samuel M'Millan. George and Robert King: Aberdeen, 1848.

Footnotes and spelling corrections have been added by the publisher.
GLH Publishing, © 2021

ISBN:
  Paperback 978-1-64863-073-6
  Epub 978-1-64863-074-3

For information on new releases, weekly deals, and free ebooks visit
www.GLHpublishing.com

CONTENTS

Sermon I.

Yea, doubtless, and I count all things but loss, for the
excellency of the knowledge of Christ Jesus my Lord.

PHILIPPIANS iii. 8.

THE apostle, in the preceding verse, having spoken of
his privileges in his unconverted state, and told how
meanly he thought of them for Christ; doth in this go
out with full sail, in running down all things whatsoever, in comparison of Christ. In the words. Consider
how things weighed in his esteem. That which was of
the greatest weight with him, and was absolutely highest in his esteem, was the excellency of the knowledge
of Christ. That is the excellency of the practical knowledge of Christ, saving acquaintance with, and interest
in him. Next what was downweighed by it, all things;
not only his good works done in his unconverted state,
but even these really good, done by the influence of the
Holy Ghost. In a word, all things imaginable, without
Christ, he counts loss; and in comparison of Christ. We
have also his certainty in this matter. He was not in
doubt about this reckoning, but with the utmost certainty was come to a point, "Yea, doubtless."

We have a remarkable evidence of a superlative esteem of Christ; namely, that whereas he had suffered
the loss of all things for him, on a review thereof, he
counted himself no loser, but fully made up, so as he
might but win Christ. So much for a general view of the
words. More particularly, before we enter on the matter

of the text, we shall attend, *first*, to the apostle's manner; and, *secondly*, to his grand scope.

I. Let us consider the manner in which the apostle delivers himself upon this great subject. He speaks with openness, with the utmost certainty, and the greatest affection. I shall illustrate these three points in their order.

1. He openly professeth his esteem of Christ above all. He does not deliver this truth in the general, that Christ is to be preferred above all, but lays it out in his own experience, that they might see that he had good reason for what he said. This teaches us, that it becomes the saints openly and avowedly to profess their superlative esteem of Christ. It is not enough to have that esteem of him in the heart, but it should have a vent outwardly. "For with the heart man believeth unto righteousness, and with the mouth confession is made unto salvation." This confession must be made for the glory of God. One great end of our regeneration and marriage with Christ is, that we may sound forth his praise in the world. "This people," says he, "have I formed for myself, they shall shew forth my praise." If his heart has been opened to receive us, why should our mouths be shut to his praise. We have no more to render, but the calves of our lips. It serves also for the good of others, that they may fall in love with Christ. "I will make thy name to be remembered in all generations, therefore shall the people praise thee for ever." The recommendations which the saints give to Christ have often a good effect. They say that the dropping of the lily begets other lilies, so the saints beget others to Christ, by the dropping of their lives, which have an attractive virtue, 1 Pet. iii. 1, 2. The drops of their blood are generative of saints. The blood of the martyrs is the seed of the church. Yea, the very droppings of their mouths for Christ are beneficial, Song vii. 9. It is then no part of religion for persons to keep their religion to

themselves. There is much hypocritical profession; but we must not hide our love to Christ, if we have any, because of that. We must not be dumb in the cause of Christ and religion, because many give him fair words, and no more. Blessed is that professor, in whom Naphtali's blessing and Joseph's do meet, goodly words, and a fruitful bough.

Let the saints learn then to be more open mouthed for Christ. Let them commend him to others, and commend him from their own experience; first, to their fellow saints, saying, "Come, and hear, all ye that fear God, and I will declare what he hath done for my soul." O! should not Christ's friends be commending their friend one to another. This would be a most seasonable work at this day, in which religion is decaying; and if ever Christ comes again, to the spirits of his people in this land, this neglected work will be revived. O! it would be like a coal of fire, to set love to Christ in motion. Will two cold flints, striking one another, kindle a fire; how much more two, in which there is some fire. "How did our heart burn," said the disciples, "within us, while he talked with us by the way, and while he opened to us the scriptures."

Let them also commend him to strangers, Song v. 9–16. Drop a word for Christ to such, you know not what it may do. Many times a word forgotten by the speaker has been minded, with time and place: by the person to whom it was spoken in Christ's behalf, and has been like seed dropped, that has sprung up sweetly afterwards. O sirs! when we come to a death-bed, and ask ourselves what have we done, what have we spoken for Christ, we will have but a sorry reflection on it, if we do not exert ourselves more in that way than we are like to do.

Let us also speak in his cause and interest in the world. We should do that especially in those things that are opposed in our day; to be sure to hold by the truth of Christ, against all opposition, Mark viii. 38. If we esteem one highly, it is natural to take his part, and to do what we can to support his interest and honour; and if Christ have our hearts, he will get our endeavours that way also.

2. The apostle, in the text, expresseth himself with the utmost certainty, "yea, doubtless." He was not halting between two opinions, but goes with full sail, to determine in Christ's favours, upon the competition of any thing whatsoever with him: "Yea, doubtless, and I count all things," &c.

DOCTRINE. In matters of religion, we should labour to be doubtless. We should be at a point, fully resolved, at a full assurance.

This holds in these two things: *First*, In the truths of religion without us. *Secondly*, In the truth of religion within us. So Paul was doubtless in these two points. He did not doubt but he so counted and esteemed Christ above all. He as little doubted, but so counting, he counted right.

I. Then we should labour to be doubtless in the truths of religion, especially the main points of religion. "Rooted and built up in him; and established in the faith as ye have been taught, abounding therein with thanksgiving." This is necessary,

1. Because, however doubts of these may be our affliction, yet they are our sin also. Satan may be the father of them, indeed; but it is a dark and unbelieving heart which is the womb in which these doubts are conceived, and by whose breasts they are nourished. It is the filthy mire of a corrupt heart, from which doubts as a thick mist do arise, to darken the light of the truth shining in the word of God.

2. Because these doubts are enemies to faith. It is true, doubting is not altogether inconsistent with faith; namely, with the existence of faith in the soul. May it

not be said that true faith is the legs of the soul; doubts are the lameness of these legs, so that though the man may walk with them, yet he walks halting by them. And so far as they are opposite to faith, they are dishonourable to God, and impeach his truth. "He that believeth on the Son of God, hath the witness in himself: be that believeth not God, hath made him a liar; because he believeth not the record that God gave of his Son."

3. Because they are the spring of apostacy and defection from the truth. They first set men a-wavering; they are carried about with every wind of doctrine; they were never truly rooted in the truth; and after they have gone hither and thither in their principles, at last they come, in a time of temptation, to fall off altogether.

Lastly, Because they are enemies to growth in religion. A floating head makes a barren life. Like a tree that never takes with the ground, but is always loose, it cannot bring forth fruit while it is so, Eph. iv. 14, 15.

Labour then to be at a point in the truths, especially the main truths of religion. And for this cause,

1. Study the word of truth, which is God's testimony to the truth. "To the law and to the testimony; if they speak not according to this word, it is because there is no truth in them." The word of God is the only foundation of faith. You may take up things upon your own fancy, or the testimony of others, and then hold fast what you have so received. But that is not faith which is not founded on divine testimony. Hence many cannot be said to be doubtless, as to the foundation points of religion, because their belief of them is not founded on the testimony of the word of God having weight with their consciences, hence their belief of them is as a house built on sand.

2. Give up yourself to the teaching of the spirit of truth. Lay your souls down before the Lord, to be taught by his Spirit. "It is written in the prophets, And they shall be all taught of God." When Peter said to Je-

sus, "Thou art the Christ, the Son of the living God," Jesus said unto him, "Blessed art thou Simon Bar-jona: for flesh and blood hath not revealed it unto thee, but my Father which is in heaven." The Spirit of God teaches men experimentally, making them not only to see, but to feel the truth and its power upon their own hearts. He brings them "to obey from the heart that form of doctrine which is delivered unto them." Their souls are cast into the mould of it. And for this cause, there is need of much humility and self-denial, and a readiness to hear what the Lord will say. "The meek will he guide in judgment, and the meek will he teach his way."

Lastly, Walk in the truth. "If any man will do his will, he shall know of the doctrine, whether it be of God, or whether I speak of myself." There is a certain harmony betwixt the truths of God, and a tendency in them to holiness of life; so as close walking with God inspires a man with a certain relish, by which he is enabled to discern betwixt truth and error; having his spiritual senses exercised, he judgeth of them, as the mouth tastes meat. We now proceed,

II. To shew that we should labour to be doubtless as to the truth of religion within us, as to the reality of grace, and not satisfy ourselves with a continued uncertainty in that point, whether Christ hath the chief room in our heart or not. We should seek after this certainty, with respect to our personal religion.

1. Because the saints may attain to it. It is promised. "He that hath my commandments," saith Jesus, "and keepeth them, he it is that loveth me: and he that loveth me shall be loved of my Father, and I will love him, and will manifest myself to him." It is commanded. "Wherefore the rather, brethren, give diligence to make your calling and election sure; for if ye do these things, ye shall never fall." Again, "Let us draw near with a true heart, in full assurance of faith; having our hearts sprinkled from an evil conscience, and our bod-

ies washed with pure water." Not only scripture saints, as David, Hezekiah, Thomas, Peter, Paul, but even many others of lower size have attained it.

2. Because doubts in this case are hurtful. Such doubts are like thistles among corn; though it is possibly not the worst ground on which they grow, yet they are hurtful weeds, and are to be plucked up. Doubts are injurious to God, and spoil him of his praise. They are injurious to the saints themselves, spoiling them of their comfort, strength, and confidence, which they might otherwise have, 2 Peter i. 10. A doubting Christian is always a weak Christian; therefore I will add,

Lastly, The case of our day calls for it. There is so little doubt of our being put to the trial, that we should now be labouring to be doubtless about it. For a doubting Christian is very unfit to act for Christ in a difficult time, and more unfit to suffer for Christ. When we have nothing in the world sure, we should endeavour to have our religion sure. Therefore in suffering or difficult times, the Lord useth to give this assurance to his people, as to Moses, Paul, &c.

DIRECTIONS. 1. Labour to get out of an ill frame, if you would be doubtless as to your state. It is difficult for a man to know in what state he is, when asleep; so in the spiritual state of security, our evidences sleep with us; therefore, awake. Nor can a man judge of his state when in a faint; so in the spiritual faint of desertion, we are not fit to read our evidences, when the light of the Lord's countenance is gone out with us. Nor can a man judge of his state, when stunned with a sore fall: thus also spiritual falls, especially relapses, put a man out of his spiritual senses. As a man when he is in a thicket of thorns, so are men sometimes in temptations, they are no sooner out, than they are taken hold of again. Wrestle then to get out of entangling temptations.

2. Labour to have a close walk with God. "Herein," says Paul, "do I exercise myself, to have a conscience

void of offence towards God and toward men." This hath the promise of assurance. "Whose offereth praise glorifieth me: and to him that ordereth his conversation aright, will I shew the salvation of God." Such a conversation makes conscience our friend, and cherisheth the Spirit, by which we are sealed. "Beloved, if our heart condemn us not, then have we confidence toward God."

3. Attend carefully to the duty of self-examination. "Examine yourselves whether ye be in the faith; prove your ownselves; know ye not your own selves, how that Jesus Christ is in you, except ye be reprobates." God has given us, in his word, marks of the soul's being in Christ, these we should apply.

Lastly, Cry much to God for his Spirit, to teach you to know the things that are freely given to you of God, and for his Spirit "to bear witness with your spirit, that you are his children."

Having thus seen the apostle openly professing his esteem of Christ above all, and expressing himself with the utmost certainty; we go on, *thirdly*, to observe that the apostle delivers himself here very affectionately, and with an enlarged heart. The more he speaks of Christ, he still riseth the higher. Some things he counted loss, but here all things; not only loss, but dung. Now,

This teacheth us, that the excellency of Christ is a subject that natively fires a gracious heart. It doth this,

1. Because all their hopes are in him. Whatever they have in hand, or in hope, of pardon, peace, joy, assurance, all is built on him as the foundation. "For they are dead, and their life is hid with Christ in God. When Christ, who is their life, shall appear, then shall they also appear with him in glory."

2. Because all their desires are in him. "Whom have I in heaven but thee, and there is none on earth that I desire besides thee." He is to them a satisfying portion, in whom they see enough to satisfy, and to give rest to their spirits.

USE 1. It is a sad symptom when people's spirits are not affected with the preaching of Christ. When people find their hearts touched and affected with the thunderings of the law, but remain unmoved with the still small voice of the gospel. When things relating to the public raise their spirits, and the preaching of Christ is tasteless to them, as the white of an egg; it is the sign either of a dead, or a distempered soul.

2. Let the saints then think, speak, and hear of Christ, as the best way to fire their coldrife[1] hearts and affections. It is by him alone we partake of divine influences; and to his saints, "his name will ever be as ointment poured forth, therefore do the virgins love him." The more the soul thinks on him, the more precious will he be in its eyes; for he is an object that will abide a look.

II. Let us consider the grand scope of the apostle in this verse. It is to shew the incomparable excellence of Christ. Every clause in the text breathes out this. "Yea, doubtless, and I count all things but loss, for the excellency of the knowledge of Jesus Christ my Lord."

DOCTRINE. Jesus Christ is an absolutely matchless one. He is a nonsuch.[2] All sheaves must bow to his. The subject of the matchless excellence of Christ, is a subject that can never be exhausted. I shall only drop a few things. There are three ways to prove the transcendent excellence of Christ.

I. By testimony.
II. By real evidence.
III. By comparison.

I. By testimony. Heaven and earth concur to bear witness to the transcendent excellence of Christ. He hath,

---

1   Cold, chilling.

2   A person who is regarded as perfect or excellent.

1. God's testimony. The Father declares him to be his delight, Isa. xlii. 1. He gave him to the world as the greatest demonstration of his love, John iii. 16. He declared by a voice from heaven, "that he is his Son, in whom he is well pleased;" not only with himself, but with sinners for his sake. This was done with great solemnity, "for lo! the heavens were opened to him, and he saw the Spirit of God descending like a dove, and lighting upon him."

2. The testimony of angels. An angel brought the news of his birth, and an host of them sung for joy at the great event, Luke ii. 10–14. In another place, we find thousands of thousands of them, giving their testimony to him, in these words: "Worthy is the Lamb that was slain, to receive power, and riches, and wisdom, and strength, and honour, and glory, and blessing."

3. The testimony of the saints in heaven, who have got a place among them that stand before the throne. This we may learn from that which is borrowed from their practice, to shew the exercise of the church militant. "They rest not day and night, saying Holy, holy, holy, Lord God Almighty, which was, and is, and is to come. They fall down before him that sitteth upon the throne, and worship him that liveth for ever." They cast their crowns before the throne, saying, "Thou art worthy, O Lord, to receive glory, and honour, and power: for thou hast created all things, and for thy pleasure they are, and were created." Could we have access to them, they would give us that testimony of him which the queen of Sheba gave of Solomon. "Behold the half was not told me: thy wisdom and prosperity exceedeth the fame which I heard. Happy are thy men; happy are these thy servants, which stand continually before thee, and hear thy wisdom."

4. The testimony of the saints on earth, who concur in this, that he is a matchless one. "Thou art fairer," say they, "than the children of men; grace is poured into

thy lips: therefore God hath blessed thee for ever." Says Asaph, "Whom have I in heaven but thee, and there is none upon earth that I desire besides thee." Says Solomon, "For wisdom is better than rubies; and all the things that may be desired, are not to be compared to it." But why should we stand upon particulars, all have given a real testimony, in joining with Paul, in the text. They know him, and therefore their testimony is to be regarded.

5. His very enemies bear testimony to him. We hear them say, Never man spake like this man.

All that profess his name, give him that testimony, though, alas! many of them, indeed, prefer others to him.

II. By real evidence, whereof take these following:

1. He is God. "He is the true God, and eternal life;" therefore his excellence is infinite. "In him dwelleth all the fulness of the Godhead bodily." "He is the brightness of his Father's glory, and the express image of his person, upholding all things by the word of his power." Angels and men, and all their works, are but created things, the workmanship of his hands. He is the Creator, the beginning: "All things were made by him; and without him was not any thing made that was made."

2. Christ is commensurate to the desires of the soul, which all creatures, conjunctly or severally, are not. All things besides him have the bounds of their goodness; one of them is good for one thing, another for another; none of them for all things. But there is an universal fitness in him, "for it pleased the Father, that in him should all fulness dwell." He is the storehouse, from which all the saints, from Adam, have derived the supply of their wants. "In him are hid all the treasures of wisdom and knowledge." What would we have, it is all in him.

3. Whatever excellency or perfection is in any thing else, it is derived from him. The most desirable crea-

tures shine with light borrowed from him. There is no perfection in the creature, but what is eminently in himself, as the first cause. "That was the true Light, which lighteth every man that cometh into the world."

4. All things beside Christ cannot make a man happy; but the enjoyment of Christ alone can do it. There are two things wanting in all the creatures, that are to be found in him. These are, *First*, sufficiency; nothing can make one happy, but what is completely satisfactory; for if there be the least want, it mars happiness; now nothing besides Christ is such. In the most prosperous condition there is something wanting, as in paradise. Christ alone is completely satisfactory, Psal. lxxiii. 25. "He is all in all;" virtually all things. He is the heir of all, and they who have him, have all. *Secondly*, certainty; what is liable to change cannot make men happy; but all things beside Christ arc so, Prov. xxiii. 5; but he is unchangeable, "the same yesterday, to-day, and forever." All fulness dwells in him; they that enjoy him need fear no change; not in this life, "for he loves unto the end;" nor in the life to come, "for they shall be ever with the Lord." No change with respect to the subject, they shall never be taken from him, Rom. viii. 38; nor with respect to the object, he shall never be taken from them.

5. When no other thing can make help to a man, Psal. cxlii. 3, 4. Thus while the cisterns of created comforts run dry, the saints live in, and by him. Thus when David was spoiled of all, in Ziklag, "he encouraged himself in the Lord his God." Thus Habakkuk resolved, that whatever should befall him, "he would rejoice in the Lord, and joy in the God of his salvation." So when death comes, they have him "to be the strength of their hearts, and portion for ever."

Lastly, He can do for us what no other can do, procure for us pardon of sin, peace with God, a right to heaven, things which angels and men cannot do.

III. By comparison. No person, no thing is to be compared with him.

1. Men on earth; what are they, in comparison of Christ. Great men; they are all but his vassals, who is King of kings; they have but a borrowed glory. Wise men; their wisdom is but folly, in comparison of the wisdom of God. Good men; their goodness is nothing, in comparison of him.

2. Saints in heaven; what are they, but so many bright stars shining with light from the Sun of Righteousness, wonders of his mercy, and monuments of his love. They are like the lilies, wearing a glory for which they never toiled.

3. Angels are all servants. He is their head. When an angel was offered to go before the people, Moses was not content, but said, "If thy presence go not with me, carry me not up hence."

4. The devils have great power: the god of this world. Christ hath the devils in a chain.

No things are to be compared with him, no affluence of worldly things. They are all of them greater in expectation than in enjoyment. All broken cisterns that soon run dry. All bitter sweets. All insufficient to satisfy the heart.

Even spiritual things are not to be compared to him. Grace and glory are his gifts; but the giver must be above the gift.

USE 1. They have a poor portion who are without Christ. They never can be happy.

2. They have made a good choice that have received Christ. Be their case what it will, they have no reason to complain; Christ is theirs. Though they have little in hand, they have much in hope.

3. We are to stand on nothing, so as we may gain Christ; and to be satisfied with nothing, if so we must lose him.

This subject reproves all the slighters of Christ. Such are profane persons, carnal worldlings, moralists, hypocrites however refined, and all such as undervalue the glory, honour, kingdom and interest of Christ in the world.

Let what hath been said commend Christ to us all.

ALL THINGS BUT LOSS FOR THE EXCELLENCY, &C.

I COME now particularly to the words. Here is the excellency of the knowledge of Christ, held forth as before all things. What is meant by the knowledge of Christ? By the knowledge of Christ here, I understand a saving interest in, and enjoyment of Christ. So it is taken, "This is life eternal, that they might know thee the only true God, and Jesus Christ whom thou hast sent." So our Lord tells the foolish virgins, "I say unto you I know you not." They plead an interest in him, hereby he disowns them as none of his. And so "seeing of God," Matth. v. 8, and "seeing of the kingdom of God," John iii. 3, is put for an interest in, and enjoying of God. And so the text must be understood; for certainly it is not the notional, speculative knowledge of Christ, which Paul's adversaries here neglected not; but the saving, practical, experimental knowledge of him, as is evident from the context, ver. 9. This is that for which he throws away all things else, taking and desiring to have him instead of all. And this is called the knowledge of Christ,

Because Christ is a spiritual object; an object for the soul, and not for the senses; "whom, having not seen, we love." The soul must rise from sensible things and occupy itself in the contemplation of his perfections, uniting with him, so that the soul finds that sweetness in him that satiates it, so that the happiness of heaven consists in the seeing of God and of Christ, "whom we shall see as he is;" that is, the enjoying of them.

DOCTRINE 1. That only is the true knowledge of Christ which terminates in an interest in, and enjoyment of him. All other knowledge that comes short of this is unworthy of the name. As the least brook that is, however shallow, differs from the deepest standing pool, while it runs into the sea, and resteth not till it be there; so the least measure of saving knowledge differs from all the light a hypocrite hath, in that it terminates in an embracing of, and uniting with Christ, while the other stands idle and inefficacious in that matter. To confirm this, consider,

1. That all the knowledge of Christ which men have, that brings them not to him, is but splendid ignorance, according to the word. Hence they are branded everywhere as fools; men whose hearts cannot be right, because their heads are not right; foolish builders, foolish virgins; they are blind also. Some persons can talk so as they are admired of the ignorant, but when knowing persons come to try their knowledge, they find they do not understand what they speak, nor whereof they affirm. So is it with those that have not the saving knowledge of Christ; their knowledge is but gilded ignorance.

2. That knowledge of Christ, which issues not in an interest in him, is not so much knowledge, as mere opinion; which is dubious and uncertain. "The natural man receiveth not the things of the Spirit of God, for they are foolishness unto him; neither can he know them, because they are spiritually discerned." Natural men, to speak properly, have not the knowledge of Christ, though they can preach him; but only an opinion, a good opinion of him, as men have of many points that are in controversy, in which they are far from an absolute certainty. They think well of Christ, but yet they will not commit themselves to him, because they are not sure. When you meet with a stranger at an inn when travelling, you find, perhaps, the man a very discreet person, and you form a good opinion of him, that he is a very honest man, and therefore you will converse with him a while; but yet you will not commit

your money to him, because though you have a very good opinion of him, he is a stranger to you, you do not know him. Just so it is with those who have only a speculative knowledge of Christ. They do not know him so well as to put their trust in him. There are two points of saving knowledge, by which I may exemplify this.

1. The superlative worth and excellency of Christ. That he is more precious than all things else, as in the text; and that all the things that may be desired are not to be compared to him. Now, no doubt, each in this congregation would answer, if asked, that they know this. But mistake it not, there is a difference betwixt knowledge and opinion. As for most of us, it is but opinion, not knowledge, otherwise we would take him for, and instead of all, Matth. xiii. 45, 46. If one should offer a pearl to an ordinary merchant for all that he hath, his attention would be excited, his heart and eye would be in the pearl indeed, but he dare not venture on the bargain; for though he has some notion that perhaps that one pearl is better than all the goods he hath, yet he is not sure. But should a jeweller come and tell him, assuring him that it is worth double of all his ware, he would take it, and give up all his ware with heart and good will. Thus saith Jesus, "if thou knewest the gift of God, and who it is that saith to thee, Give me to drink; thou wouldest have asked of him, and he would have given thee living water."

2. Christ's sufficiency. That Christ is able to bear all the sinner's weight for time and eternity. That he is just such an high priest as became us. We all think we know this; and certainly the saints that have believed, and rolled all their weight upon him, have known it. They can say, each for himself, "I know whom I have believed, and am persuaded that he is able to keep that which I have committed to him against that day." But really, to the most part, it goes no farther than a bare

opinion, which never brings them to venture all freely upon him. They are like a man fallen into a deep pit, a rope is let down, he looks to it again and again, thinks it is strong enough; yet when he comes to try it, he starts back, cannot venture for he is not sure, and therefore falls a climbing up, till he fall and ruin himself. Now the true knowledge of Christ differs exceedingly from this opinion of him. Says Paul to the Thessalonians, "Knowing, brethren beloved, your election of God. For our Gospel came not unto you in word only, but also in power, and in the Holy Ghost, and in much assurance."

3. The true knowledge of Christ engages the heart, and captivates the soul. "And they that know thy name, will put their trust in thee; for thou, Lord, hast not forsaken them that seek thee." When the gospel comes in power and demonstration of the Spirit, the heart of a sinner is overpowered, that as it cannot hinder itself to assent to clear truth, so it cannot but embrace him as the chief good. "Because of the savour of thy good ointments, thy name is as ointment poured forth, therefore do the virgins love thee." As the loadstone draws iron to it, so there is a divine virtue in spiritual illumination, to draw the sinner to Christ. As some waters have a healing virtue coming through minerals, so Christ, riding in triumph in his glory through the soul, certainly gains the heart consent of those that behold him. So that that light, like the fire of the furnace, burns off the children's bonds wherewith they were held before.

4. The saving knowledge of Christ differs not in kind, but in degrees, from heaven's happiness. It is the commencement of eternal life in the soul, John xvii. 3, "But we all with open face beholding as in a glass the glory of the Lord, are changed into the same image, from glory to glory, even as by the Spirit of the Lord." Here the knowledge of him is through a glass darkly, there face to face. As in heaven, then, there is a complete happiness and enjoyment of God, from that knowledge

of him there; so there is a real interest and enjoyment of him here, in some, in which the knowledge of him here doth issue. What did it avail the rich man, to see Abraham, and Lazarus in his bosom, afar off; this contributed to his torment. So what avails any knowledge of Christ, without an interest in him? As James says of faith without works, "Can faith save you?" So may we say of mere speculative knowledge, Can it save you?

Lastly, The true knowledge of Christ is not an idle speculation, but a practical experimental knowledge, ver. 9. It is to know him, that we may be partakers of him. Saving knowledge is transforming, 2 Cor. iii. 18. Men do not dig into the bowels of the earth to see gold, but to enjoy it; nor do they know the treasure in Christ, whose business it is not to make it their own.

USE 1. Of Information.

1. Many of those who want not knowledge of the truths of religion in some sort, may begin again to learn the A, B, C, of Christian knowledge. How many learned ignorants are there in the world, that know something of all things, but the one thing needful. This is a certain rule. A man has no more of Christ in his head, than he has of him in his heart. And if that be so truly, for as far as most of us are on, we may be brought back to the first question of grace's catechism, "What is his name, and what is his Son's name, if thou canst tell?"

2. True knowledge carries a man out of himself to Christ, and so fills a man with humility and self-denial. "I have heard of thee by the hearing of the ear," says Job, "but now mine eye seeth thee, wherefore I abhor myself, and repent in dust and ashes." That knowledge which puffeth up is none of the right sort, for were it of the right kind, it would, as a river, run into the sea of the excellency of Christ, and raise him, and empty and humble men's selves in their own eyes. No more knowledge of Christ have we, than we have of humility

and self-denial. They to whom Christ is all, will themselves be nothing in their own eyes.

3. Surely Christ is a veiled beauty to those who are not interested in him. They that know him cannot but love and embrace him, they cannot refuse him. If Christ has not yet got thy heart, surely thine eyes are held, that thou canst not perceive him, Song v. 9–16, compare chap. vi. 1. Thou couldst not prefer any thing to him, if thou didst but behold his glory, therefore thou knowest no more of him than he has of thy heart.

4. In whatever measure any thing besides Christ carries away the heart, the knowledge of Christ is so far lost. The heart of man is an empty thing that must needs be seeking satisfaction in the enjoyment of something. If thy heart be inordinately going out after the enjoyment of the creatures, it is an evidence that it has so far lost the knowledge of his excellence; so far as that is gone, so far hast thou lost the true knowledge of him. And, therefore, for recovery, turn the eyes of thy mind towards him to behold his glory, which is the readiest way to darken created excellence.

Lastly, The best way to obtain true knowledge of Christ, is to be much in seeking and conversing with him, that is the way to enjoy him. "My soul shall be satisfied as with marrow and fatness, and my mouth shall praise thee with joyful lips, when I remember thee upon my bed, and meditate on thee in the night watches." "If any man will do his will, he shall know of the doctrine, whether it be of God, or whether I speak of myself." Practical religion is the best way to attain to more of the knowledge of Christ. As those with whom we would be acquainted, we must be much in their company, and converse with them frequently; so this is the way in which Christians get the secrets of the covenant manifested to them.

USE 2. Let me exhort you to labour to know Christ, and to improve your knowledge of him to an interest in, and enjoyment of him; and never satisfy yourselves with a knowledge of him that comes short of that. Never reckon you know more than you enjoy and feel in your souls of Christ, or than you really, in believing, make use of, and improve for your souls. Consider,

1. Such knowledge is very useless to you, whatever it may be to others, for whom God can serve himself of it, to lead them in the way of truth. What would it avail a man to know the remedy, while he neglects to apply it; would not such an one die of his disease. Sinners, what will it avail you, that you know Christ is a Saviour, if you do not employ him? What the better is a man, that he dies within sight of the physician? What would it avail if a man had ever so much knowledge of the law, if yet he suffer men to wheedle him out of his estate, while he neglects to plead his right? And what though you know what to do to be saved, if you do it not? What the better are you to know Christ to be an up-making portion, if you take him not for your portion?

2. Nay, such knowledge is noxious. It doth for the present aggravate your sin. Sins against light, are of all sins the most heavy. For the future, it will aggravate your condemnation. Alas! what is that knowledge, that serves only as a lantern to light men into everlasting darkness?

3. Our disease lies more in our hearts than in our heads. There was some knowledge left after the fall, Rom. ii. 15; but there was no goodness, no heart holiness. If physic be taken, yet if it do not operate to carry off the ill humours of the body, a person is nothing the better, but rather the worse; so is it when knowledge comes into the head, but sinks not into the heart. Men's minds should usher in the truth received, into the heart; but instead of that, they are often as jailors, to lock it up in prison that it cannot stir, "They hold the truth in unrighteousness."

Lastly, God will not own his knowing of any, but those in whom he has a special interest, Matth. xxv. 12. And if ye would reckon as God will do, you would reckon thus also.

USE 3. Of comfort to those that have seen as much of Christ, as that they cannot rest without an interest in him; and have some enjoyment of him, but may be discouraged under a sense of weakness of knowledge. But be comforted, it is true knowledge. And as a little gold is far more precious than much brass, so the lowest degree of true knowledge is far better than great stores of mere speculative knowledge.

DOCTRINE II. All things are but loss in comparison of an interest in Christ, and the enjoyment of him. This is a point that runs counter to the judgment of all the unregenerate world, who count highly of other things, but make light of Christ and an interest in him. This is confirmed by the daily practice of all out of Christ. Here I shall,

I. Shew in what respects all things are but loss in comparison of an interest in Christ, and the enjoyment of him.

II. I shall confirm this point by proofs and illustrations. I am then,

I. To show in what respects all things are but loss, in comparison of an interest in Christ, and the enjoyment of him.

1. There is not one thing in all the creation, but it is loss, in comparison of the enjoyment of Christ as ours. Turn over all the creatures, and all created perfections in the world, single out the best of them, and the most desirable, take the choicest, it will be but refuse in comparison of Christ.

2. All of them together, are but loss in this respect. Suppose you were possessed of the whole inventory of good things; profitable pleasant things, lawful and

unlawful, that what is wanting in one, may be made up to you in another; lay the possession of them in one balance, and the enjoyment of Christ in another, they would all be weighed down. If the whole constellation of created perfections should arise upon you, Christ, as the Sun of Righteousness, would darken them all. Had you Solomon's riches and wisdom, Samson's strength, Absalom's beauty; should all the created comforts ever man had, or ever will have, fall down together into your bosom, all would be nothing in comparison of an interest in Christ, and the enjoyment of him. All is but loss. All are of no value in comparison of an interest in Christ. The best of them are not worthy to be named with him in one day. Health and strength are good, and outward accommodations and privileges are good, but as the glorious stars hide their heads when the sun appears, so must all these things before Christ. They are all to be thrown away, when we cannot have Christ with them. If it comes to that, that we must part with Christ or part with them, then we have reason to say, farewell profits, pleasures, honours, liberty, life itself, and all things, and welcome Christ. They are to be lost in that case, but in no case must we agree to lose him. The man is at no loss that loseth them, but gains Christ. He loseth but loss, which no man will grudge. He is sufficiently made up in the want of them all, by the enjoyment of Christ.

Finally, He has a poor bargain of it, that has all, but wants Christ. His gain may be soon told, his loss cannot be reckoned up. We now proceed,

II. To confirm this point by proofs and illustrations. O to believe it! The belief of it would turn the current of our desires and endeavours another way.

1. An interest in Christ makes God ours, for he is God; "the fulness of the Godhead dwells in him." So runs the covenant, in which God makes over himself, in Christ, to sinners: "I will," says he, "be to them a God,

and they shall be to me a people." He is their portion and their heritage. They are children and heirs, "heirs of God, and joint heirs with Christ." Now what is all the world in comparison of God himself? While others can say, this land, this house is mine, the Christian can say, God is mine, for Christ is mine: "Lo this God is our God." An interest in Christ, then, is absolutely the greatest treasure. Men nor angels cannot make an inventory of the Christian's portion, which is summed up in this, God is theirs. The greatest abundance of earthly things maybe reckoned, and you will soon hear that there is no more. "But eye hath not seen, nor ear heard, neither have entered into the heart of man, the things which God hath prepared for them that love him." The infinite perfections of God are their treasure, and this treasure will tell out to all eternity. It is also absolutely the most valuable treasure, for what proportion can there be betwixt the perfections of God, and those of the creature. Worldly men may have some streams of good things let out to them, but the Christian has the fountain of all. Now, where the water is good, it is best in the spring. Sure then the enjoyment of God must be best. God's goodness, love, and all-sufficiency is theirs.

2. An interest in Christ is the one thing necessary. "One thing" says our Lord, "is needful." All things must go for necessaries. A man parts with his money and goods for his health, and will part with all for his life. He reckons all nothing in comparison of that, because he can live without other things, but none of these things can avail him, if he lose his life, Matth. vi. 25. Even so an interest in Christ stands by itself, and is not to be reckoned among, but above all things else.

Other things are conveniencies to be thankfully received, but not necessaries that cannot be wanted. Man's great desire is to be happy. This is the end which all propose to themselves. Now, I say, other things besides Christ are not absolutely necessary for this end.

It is not necessary that you may be rich, you may be happy without riches. Lazarus was happy, though poor; the apostles, though despised, and counted as the off-scouring of all; Job, without either health or wealth; the saints in heaven are stripped of the comforts of this life, yet perfectly happy; therefore happiness may be without them.

But an interest in Christ is absolutely necessary. No happiness without it. Though you were compassed about with all the profits and pleasures of the world, yet in this case the sword of vengeance hangs above thy head. Thou art but as a condemned malefactor set down at a well covered table, but knoweth not how soon he may be raised and led to execution. Though the earth smiles on thee, yet heaven frowns; though men bless, God curseth thee, and may say to thee, "thou fool, this night shall thy soul be required of thee; then whose shall those things be which thou hast provided?"

Again, nothing can make up the want of an interest in Christ; but an interest in him can make up the want of all things else. All the gold of the Indies will not buy a pardon, nor the greatest earthly honours keep from everlasting contempt. Have what you will, if you have not Christ, you are under a loss that cannot be made up another way; but that makes up all other wants, Philip. iv. 18. Whatever you want, if Christ be yours, you have what is better.

Finally, Every thing that one really needs is comprehended in it, so that the way to get all our needs compendiously answered, is to get an interest in Christ. Our wants are far more than our needs. We reckon our needs more than they are; but once in Christ; then one may well expect to get all he really needs made out to him. "He that spared not his own son, but delivered him up for us all, how shall he not with him also freely give us all things." "For the Lord will give grace and glory; no good thing will he withhold from them that walk uprightly." Whatever his people need, God, as a Father, will provide for them, Matth. vi. 32.

3. An interest in Christ is satisfying to the soul, while nothing else can give satisfaction. You may as soon grasp your arms full of dreams, and embrace your own shadow, as suck satisfaction out of the dry breasts of the creatures. But in Christ there is what will satisfy the soul, answer its desires in breadth and length. There are two things necessary to give satisfaction. *First*, Suitableness. Now Christ is a suitable enjoyment for the soul. He is suitable to the nature of the soul, which is spiritual, and the enjoyment of him is the enjoyment of spiritual blessings. "God blesses us with all spiritual blessings in heavenly places in Christ." The soul is immortal, and so an interest in Christ is durable; "for durable riches and righteousness are with him." He is suitable to the necessities of the soul, for pardon, peace, and every blessing; whereas all things of the world are nothing so.

Again, fulness is necessary to satisfaction. Now there is a fulness of these suitable blessings in him. "It hath pleased the Father, that in him should all fulness dwell." What can be wanting in an infinite good. Here then "we eat that which is good, and our souls delight themselves in fatness."

4. An interest in Christ is the most enriching interest. Were an estimate to be made of what the meanest Christian is worth, and what the richest monarch, the Christian's would be found infinitely beyond his. The Christian has a right to more, for he hath a right to all through Christ. "All things," says Paul to believers, "are yours." The Christian has married the heir of all things, and so may set his name on all that is his. What though he hath but little in hand, yet look his papers, read his charter, his bonds under the hand of God himself, containing the promises of this life and that which is to

come, and the greatest riches of the graceless world, is rank poverty in comparison of that.

Nay, the Christian hath more in actual possession than the greatest on earth. The most precious and valuable riches are ordinarily least in bulk. A little gold, or a small pearl, is more valuable than a bag full of brass coin. Reckon thus, and the man that is interested in Christ hath more in hand than the richest in the world. His grace is more precious than gold, his power over his own spirit better than dominion over kingdoms. What is so great on earth as a kingdom? What kingdom so great as that of heaven? The Christian has it: "For behold the kingdom of God is within you." And this leads us to observe, that the Christian, by his interest in Christ, hath all within himself, that he needs not go out for it. You will say such a man has a well furnished house and table, some things he got from such a place, and some things from another. O! but, say you, there is another man hath all things within himself, the last is preferable. So in this. What an ungodly man doth most value, generally it is without himself. His riches are in his coffers, his plenty in his barns, his dominion is given him by others, and can be taken away; his honour also depends on others. But the Christian hath all within himself, because Christ is in him. Yes, "Christ is in him, the hope of glory." "A good man," it is said, "shall be satisfied from himself." Christians "know in themselves, that they have in heaven a better and an enduring substance." He hath a kingdom within, that contains what is suitable for every case.

Here, also, I would remark, that the little that one hath, that hath an interest in Christ, is more valuable than the greatest abundance of a Christless man. "A little," saith the Psalmist, "that a righteous man hath, is better than the riches of many wicked." Better than the riches, even than the riches of many. But how can that be? I answer, the little they have, they have it with the love of God; and whatever others have, they have it with his wrath and anger. "The curse of the Lord is in the house of the wicked, but he blesseth the habitation of the just." What the Christian hath, comes from God's love, and is a token of his love; and you know tokens are valued more for the sake of the giver, than the gift itself.

Again, the Christian hath the sanctified use of what he possesses. All that they have comes to them through the channel of the covenant, and tends to their good. "For we know that all things work together for good to them that love God, to them who are the called according to his purpose," whereas others, by virtue of a secret curse that is in what they have, are thereby injured. There is death in the pot. "The prosperity of fools shall destroy them." Many have been nourished and supported with coarse fare, when kings and emperors have had poison mixed with their most delicious meats. So it is here.

Besides, the little that the Christian hath, he hath it freely, nothing to pay. It is paid for already by the blood of Christ. But others will have a dear reckoning that will pay for all at the latter end. They may write on all their enjoyments this motto, The price of blood. "For what is a man profited, if he shall gain the whole world, and lose his own soul? or what shall a man give in exchange for his soul?" The world is as a commodious inn, perhaps the children there do not fare so well as the stranger. But then the stranger gets his bill ere he go away, when he must pay dear for all he hath got.

The Christian, also, hath a far better right to his little, than the other hath to his abundance. A covenant right, it is the purchase of Christ. It was precious water that was brought to David, out of the well of Bethlehem, more precious than wine, because it was the price of blood.

Others have but a right by common providence. Their good things are bones cast to dogs. It is but as a supper which a malefactor enjoys before he is led forth to execution.

Lastly, The little which the Christian hath, is an earnest of more mercy. You may call it Joseph, for God will add another to it. Now, a little given as an earnest, is better by far than a great sum, after which no more is to be expected. Even the Christian's wants are better than the abundance of others, even as the want of strong liquor is better than to have it to put us in a fever.

5. An interest in Christ is the only abiding, lasting interest. It will abide when we must lose all other things. We see that a little thing coming in yearly, is preferred to great sums in hand, which may soon be all spent. An interest in Christ cannot be taken from us as other things may, Matth. vi. 19. The philosopher called riches the vomit of fortune; if so, we find the vomit is often resumed. Job in his time saw himself rich and poor to a proverb, Prov. xxiii. 5. But once in Christ, always in him. The landed man may have his crop destroyed, but his land abides. Other things are lent us, but this is an irrevocable gift.

We cannot be taken from it, Matth. vi. 20. The man that dies interested in Christ is his own heir, and carries his interest into another world with him. The worldly comforts men have, are like servants in an inn, that wait upon persons while they continue there, but go not away with them, but abide to serve others that come after them.

Lastly, I shall prove it by an induction of particulars upon which men set their hearts more than upon Christ.

1. Knowledge of other things besides Christ, is no way comparable to the knowledge of Christ. The pleasure which men find in it, is infinitely below that which they find in the knowledge of Christ. It can do no good

at death, and they will have no more use for it through eternity, while the other will continue as the saint's eternal happiness. "This is life eternal, that they might know thee the only true God, and Jesus Christ whom thou hast sent." They are like men going through a city, gazing at every thing about them, while they never look to their own way, and neglect their own business. Each of them may say with Grotius, Ah! I have destroyed life, laboriously doing nothing.

2. Riches are vain, and, laid in the balance with an interest in Christ, are lighter than vanity. They are uncertain as the wind, and can never fill the heart, Prov. xxiii. 5. Nay, they enlarge the desires, where grace does not narrow them; for worldliness is a sort of spiritual drunkenness, that the more one gets, the more he would have.

They cannot profit in the day of wrath. It is with Christians and others, as with Abraham's children. Abraham gave all that "he had unto Isaac. But unto the sons of the concubines which Abraham had, he gave gifts, and sent them away from Isaac his son." Christians are with the first, they are heirs; others get but moveables, and they are made over to them with the burden of danger, for saith Jesus "how hardly shall they that have riches enter into the kingdom of God." There is danger in an evil time from men by them. The tall oaks are torn up by the roots, while the low shrubs escape; and they are at all times, but especially in evil times, a snare to the soul. They are a handle by which Satan holds men; so that while they cleave to them, Satan draws them to himself. They have also a burden of duties. God requires more of rich persons than of others. "To whom much is given, from them much shall be required." They have accounts to give. They are but stewards, and the more they have among their hands, their accounts will be the greater, Luke xvi. But an interest in Christ shall never be lost.

3. Honour and reputation. What vain things are they, depending upon the uncertain thoughts of others; and where men have them at many hands, they may be wanting at that hand where they might do them most good. How easily is reputation stained, and it is at the mercy of every calumnious detractor. It is a windy bubble of water that has no solidity in it, and quickly is gone. But he that has an interest in Christ, though he should lie among the pots while he lives here, shall shine in that honour which is eternal, hereafter.

4. An easy and pleasant life in the world is a vain thing, much desired and pursued, to the neglect of an interest in Christ. But let us do our utmost to make our bed soft here, there shall ever be found some thorn of uneasiness in it. No sound ease but in Christ. When world's ease is got, it bears hard on the soul, which as readily corrupts; while troubles in the world set men to their duty. And how suddenly is men's ease and pleasure interrupted; and the more they had of it, they can the worse bear the want of it.

5. Friends able to do one a kindness are much valued. They that have them, value themselves upon them; they that want them, think they would be well if they had them. But alas! how oft do they prove like brooks dried up, Job vi. 15; and how quickly may we be in such a case, that if even our best friends were never so willing, they are utterly unable to help us. Christ is a friend that can, and will help in all cases.

6. Comfortable relations; a husband, wife, or children, dutiful and comfortable. Great mercies indeed, but loss in comparison of an interest in Christ. How difficult is it for us to have them such and not make gods of them? How difficult to rejoice, and not overjoy in them? And many times where people have thought to find their greatest comfort, there they have found their greatest cross. And however comfortable, yet they must

part; and when they go, the more comfortable they were, the deeper is the wound they leave behind them.

7. Liberty is what every person prizes; there is always no man who would not rather choose to be stripped of all, and to wander to find her for himself, than to be penned up in a palace. But what serves that liberty, while a man is still in the devil's chain, and has the eternal prison abiding him; that though he can go where he will, yet be can go no where but where Satan is with him, and in him. How much more worthy is an interest in Christ. Though the body be imprisoned, confined, or banished, yet the soul has access at all times to the throne of God.

8. Life is dearer than all these, yet is but loss in comparison of an interest in Christ. What a vain thing is the life of man on earth, liable to a thousand accidents, and which even a blast of infected air can take away. The lamp goes out at length, the oil being wasted; and while it remains, may be clogged with such miseries as may make life itself a burden, and men to court their dissolution, that they may rest in a grave. To none of these is an interest in Christ liable, it is that which secures an eternal life.

Lastly, In a word, self is what most men seek, neglecting Christ. But what a vain thing are we ourselves. It will not be amiss to give here some self-debasing considerations. Consider, then, we are nothing. Whatever figure we make, we are nothing; that is to say, we are worth nothing. However great, we are but fair nothings. I Am, is God's name. Take away the parts of a compound, and then it is nothing. Let God take back his own from us, and we are nothing. You will see some men make a great appearance, and you think they are rich men; but others that know their affairs will tell you that they are worth nothing, for it is all other people's property that they have among their hands; and that if every one had their own, they would be brought to nothing. "Without me," saith Jesus, "ye can do nothing." We are but mere tools in the Lord's hands: without him we can do nothing in grace or nature. As our being is from him, so is our working. Again, we deserve nothing. We are unprofitable servants. Our demerit is great, our merit nothing. We deserve hell indeed, but deserve not the least mercy. Yea, we are worse than nothing, as being sinful creatures, even as a cup full of poison is worse than an empty cup.

Use 1. Of information.

1. How foolish are men, then, who are very busy and diligent to get other things, but who neglect to get an interest in Christ. Like Martha, they are careful and troubled about many things, while they neglect the one thing needful, the better part. With what carefulness do men manage their business for their bodies, who are careless of their souls. Surely this interest is the great project we should be driving in the world, and not be seeking after that which is lost, to the neglecting of the great gain.

2. They have made but a poor purchase, have what they will, that have not an interest in Christ. Can they be happy, though they were monarchs of the world? They cannot, for their all is but a heap of loss and dung, they have nothing substantial and durable. Have what you will, what will all these things avail you, if you have not Christ.

3. The righteous is more excellent than his neighbour. The poorest saint on earth is richer than the greatest man on earth that is a Christless man. He hath that which is of more worth than all the world. O! but fretting and discontentment ill becomes a Christian for want of any worldly thing. Does not Jesus say, Am I not better to thee than ten sons. Surely it is because they see not their stock.

4. Men are no losers, lose what they will for Christ. We have no reason to grudge to suffer the loss of all for him.

Use 2. Of exhortation. I exhort you then to seek and secure an interest in Christ for yourselves. Make this your great business. I have often called you to this, and it has been the great scope of all my preaching among you to lead you to Christ. And now when the Lord is threatening to draw our table, and separate ministers from their flocks, I desire once more to call and invite you to an interest in Christ. And if I could prevail, though I should never more have access to serve you in the gospel, I would think I had got my errand.

Motive 1. Christ is willing to receive you. There is a match proposed betwixt the King of Glory and the daughter of Zion, Christ and sinners. And I declare there is nothing to hinder it on Heaven's part. "For the Spirit and the bride say, Come. And let him that heareth say, Come. And let him that is athirst come. And whosoever will, let him take of the water of life freely." Young sinners, that are setting out in the world, he is content to be yours. "I love them that love me," says he, "and they that seek me early shall find me." Old sinners, he is content to be yours, though you have refused many calls. He excludes none of you, do not, I beseech you, exclude yourselves. "Ho! every one that thirsteth, come ye to the waters; and he that hath no money, come ye, buy and eat; yea come, buy wine and milk without money and without price." And to evidence his willingness to be yours, consider,

Why did he come the long journey from heaven to earth, but to relieve the captive daughter of Zion. Are you the lost, Luke xix. 10. Why did he leave the Father's bosom, but to bring these back to it, whom sin had shaken out. Why suffered he, but that they might be saved? Why was he bruised, but that he might become bread to the hungry soul? Why shed he his blood, but to remove the lawful impediments of this match?

In vain did he shed his blood, if sinners amongst men be not partakers of it. Whom had he in his eye for reconciliation? Not angels, not devils, Heb. ii. 6. It was men, "Unto you, O men, I call; and my voice is to the sons of men." Not to the righteous, there were none such; and if there had been, they had not needed him. Answer to your name then, O sinners! for such Christ came to call; he really offers himself to you in his word preached by his ambassadors. How then can you doubt his willingness. Our offer is really, though ministerial, Christ's own offer, for we have his commission to bear us out in it. Our commission and office we had not from the magistrate, therefore it is not in their power to deprive us of it, as they may deprive men of offices civil and military, which come from them. But our commission is from Christ. We teach not but what Christ has commanded us, and therefore he will be with us in it; which these have no ground to pretend to, that teach for doctrines the commandments of men, whom this Church is in hazard of having thrust in upon her; 2 Cor. v. 20. We are proxies for the Lord of Glory, come to you with his own word, by his orders. Would you have himself leave his glory a second time, to offer himself to you? Or would you have him come in his glory. You know not what you ask. It would become you better to do, as 1 Sam. xxv. 40–41.

Our offer of him in his own name, is so really his, that you will be eternally ruined, if you refuse it, Mark xvi. 15, 16; John xvii. 20.

Consider, also, how long he has waited upon you, and after many refusals has still, and is courting your consent, Rev. iii. 20. Why did he not go away at your first or second refusal? No, but you have still line upon line. *Finally*, he knows very well what is in you and about you; yet hath he declared, that nothing shall hinder the match, if you be willing. Though you be poor and miserable, he is willing to take you, to enrich you, to clothe you, and nourish you for ever; and is he not then willing to be yours.

Motive 2. Consider what you are without him. Wretched and miserable is the state of every Christless soul. If you saw your case by the light of the Spirit, you would be much affected. Let us glance at a few parts of your picture, as it is presented in the glass of the word. Sinner, thou art God's enemy. "The carnal mind is enmity against God." Thou camest into the world in a state of enmity against God. The reconciliation is not yet made up, for there is no peace with God, but through Christ. Hast thou no interest in Christ, then what hast thou to do with peace, who hast nothing to do with the great peacemaker. There is wrath in God's heart, in his word, and in his hand against thee.

Again thou art debtor to justice. Sin is thy debt, which thou art not, and never will be able to pay. Thou art in the hand of an inexorable creditor. Thou hast no cautioner to be surety for thy debt. Thou wilt not get thy debt denied. Conscience will be instead of a thousand witnesses against thee. Thou wilt be pursued for principal and interest, and the debt will be pursued at thy own expense. Thou art also the law's criminal. God hath a law, and by that law thou must die. "For the wages of sin is death." The law condemns thee, takes away thy life as a traitor to God, an enemy to heaven. Thou livest but as a malefactor, by the benefit of a reprieve, and thou knowest not how soon it may expire.

Thou art, moreover, Satan's slave, captive, and prisoner. Thou art under "the power of Satan, and taken captive by him at his will." In this case Christ finds all those to whom he comes. Behold thy drudgery work, the sign of thy slavery, thy chains, thy captivity, thy prison garments that are on thee.

Thou, O sinner! in thy Christless state, art to every good work reprobate. Thou canst do nothing good or acceptable in the sight of God. Thy prayers are but howling, thy sacrifice an abomination, thy throat an open sepulchre.

Besides, in thy Christless state, sinner, thou art a stranger to the covenant of grace, and all the benefits of it, Eph. ii. 12. Thou hast not married the heir, and, therefore, what hast thou to do with the benefits of the contract. Thou canst have no pardon nor peace in your present state.

Thou art a burden to the earth, Rom. viii. 22. Every creature is thine enemy. The very meat which thou eatest, waits a command to dispatch thee. Thou art an abomination to heaven, that will have nothing to do with thee. "For there shall in no wise enter into it any thing that defileth, neither whatsoever worketh abomination, or maketh a lie." Thou art a prey to the pit's devouring mouth that waiteth for thee.

MOTIVE 3. An interest in Christ is the best interest which you can have in the world. Consider that it is an interest for soul and body both. A man's purchase in the world, may furnish him something in the world for his body, food and raiment, and the like; but nothing for the soul. This will furnish you peace, pardon, and all the benefits of the everlasting covenant. Yea, and for the body, it makes it a member of Christ, a temple for the Spirit, and ensures a glorious resurrection. It is an interest both for heaven and earth. It makes them to inherit the earth, Matth. v. 5, by their right to it in Christ, and their contentment with what they have of it, as if they had it all, and this interest entitles them to glory. It is then both for time and eternity. "It is profitable unto all things, having the promise of the life that now is, and that which is to come." It is the best security for a through-bearing here, and will be an interest of which you will reap the fruits for ever.

Motive 4. Consider the case of the day in which we live, calls loudly for us to secure our own interest in Christ. And we can make no good use of the reelings of the times, if they do not lead us to this. Have we not need of something which men cannot take from us? And what is that, but an interest in Christ, with the benefits depending thereon? We are threatened with persecution and with the sword, in which the Church and land were once involved, what in such a case have men they can call their own? Have we not need of something that may be comfortable to us, under the loss of all things? Indeed, the man that hath an interest in Christ may say, I have a refuge, a portion.

If you be called to suffering, what a sad thing is it to suffer for one in whom you have no interest. You will be ready to turn your back upon him; and yet, shunning suffering for a good cause, you may be brought to suffer dishonourably, whether you will or not, so as sinning will not keep you from suffering.

When snares are abroad, and a course of defection, how can you think to escape that have no interest in Christ? And when the Lord is threatening to remove the gospel from you, it calls you at length to answer his call.

Motive 5, and *last*. Let the consideration of eternity stir you up. What will you do without an interest in Christ, when death arrests you? The soul and body must part. Who will keep you from the second death? When time is gone, thou must pass to eternity.

What will you do when the resurrection comes? What hill or mountain will cover the sinner from the face of the Lamb?

When, O sinner! thou must stand before the tribunal, and that very Saviour whom thou now slightest will be thy Judge, who will then plead thy cause?

Directions. View your sinfulness. Get a deep sight of your misery without Christ, your utter inability to help yourselves, and the helplessness of all creatures. Give away yourselves solemnly to Christ, and all that is yours, taking him for, and instead of all. Amen.

Sermon II.

My Lord.

Philippians iii. 8.

Here the apostle asserts his interest in Christ, calling him his Lord; not only as Christ had an interest in him and lordship over him, but in so far as he had an interest in Christ. "My beloved is mine, and I am his."

Doctrine. Saints may, and ought to plead an interest in Christ as their Lord. The Lord's people sometimes fall into the hands of strange lords, who are hard lords to them. But in the worst of times a child of God may tell a fivefold tale of Christ, which their graceless enemies cannot. Every saint may say of Christ,

1. He is my Lord God. For as low as his work and cause are, the believer's Lord is God, and his God, John xx. 28. "The fulness of the Godhead dwells in him." "He is God manifested in the flesh." Now an interest in God as our God, is an interest above expression. His infinite wisdom is theirs to direct, his power to protect them. "Happy is that people that is in such a case; yea happy is that people whose God is the Lord." Why then should they be afraid of men, however severe masters they be?

2. My Lord, proprietor, master and owner. We and all ours are the Lord's, therefore he may dispose of us as he will, and we are to submit. In the day of the soul's closing with Christ, we gave up ourselves and all our's

39

to the Lord, and so must we say, "we are thy servant's, O Lord! truly we are thy servants." But of others, Satan is their lord and proprietor.

3. My Redeemer. "He gave himself for us, to redeem us from all iniquity." When our lives were forefeited to the justice of God, he came and bought them with his precious blood. And shall any thing be too dear to us to lose for him.

4. My Lord and husband. He sought the believer in spiritual marriage, who has consented to him, and so he is their husband. A noble relation! "For thy maker is thy husband, the Lord of Hosts is his name." And therefore it is below a child of God to prostitute himself, his soul and conscience, to the lusts of men, or pollute them to please the greatest on earth.

Lastly, My Lord and King. He has subdued them to himself. They have accepted him as their King and Lawgiver. His throne is in their hearts, and his laws are there; and therefore they can do nothing contrary to their allegiance to him, command it who will, under the most severe penalties. And in the strict observation of his laws, they may expect such protection and provision from him who is the King of kings, as he sees good for them.

The saints may plead this relation to him and interest in him, for they really have it. Though their real state be capable of degrees, and one is more holy than another, yet this honour have all the saints, and that equally. He is as much the Lord, God, Husband, and King of the meanest soever, as of the strongest. And they ought to plead it.

1. It is very pleasing to God, Jer. iii. 4. God loves to have his children know their relation to him, and therefore are the Scriptures written and the Spirit given, that we may know the things freely given us of God. We need not blame any but ourselves, if we walk in darkness. It is the weakness of our eyes that keeps us from

seeing our privileges, and it robs God of the sacrifice of praise.

2. It is very comfortable and strengthening to the saints themselves, 2 Pet. i. 10. This would not only heighten our comforts in the worst of times, but heighten our graces, our love, repentance, obedience, our trust in him, and dependence upon him.

USE I. O! the happy state of the saints, beyond all the world. Christ is theirs. *Mine* is a sweet word, especially when it is joined to the most glorious object. Nebuchadnezzar could say, my kingdom, my majesty; but my Lord and my God, is a note of an infinitely higher strain. This is a property that is above all other, that may comfort in the want of all, and will supply all other wants, and is a property which none can take from us.

2. Let the saints improve their faith to this degree of assurance, that they may confidently, though humbly, call Christ their Lord. But of this before. It is the weakness of the saints, that they dare not say, My Lord. It is no presumption in a gracious soul to say so, who has taken Christ for his Lord. Thou mayest say it.

1. If Christ be Lord of thy heart, having the chief room in thy affections, Psal. lxxiii. 25, hast thou seen a glory in him, that has darkened all created excellency, so that he reigns in thy affections, and thy heart is his captive, so that he is dearer to thee than what is dearest in the world?—call him then thy Lord, for he is Lord of thy heart.

2. If he be Lord of thy life, so that thou endeavourest continually to live to him and not to thyself, not to thy lusts, Phil. i. 21. The great design thou hast in the world is to please him, and to walk before him to all well pleasing, in heart, lip and life; and what is displeasing to him, is displeasing and a burden to thee also. Call him then thy Lord.

3. If he be Lord of thy all, so that thou art content to part with all that is dear to thee rather than with him,

his favour, his truths, his work, and cause, Luke xiv. 26. If thou hast laid down thy all at his feet, to be disposed of what way he will, call him then Lord.

Lastly, Let the people of God follow their duty to Christ as their Lord, in spite of all opposition from the world. If the commands of men go cross to the commands of Christ, though they were the highest powers on earth, let us remember we are to obey our Lord God rather than men; and let us never do a thing to please our lords on earth, that will displease our Lord from heaven. This day, alas! is a day in which the commands of our rulers on the ministry of this Church cannot be obeyed in the judgment of many worthy ministers, without disobeying our great Lord and Master; though others are not of that mind. This threatens to rend this Church asunder, to separate ministers from their flocks, and to shut up many kirk doors, and yours among the rest. Prepare for snares, and cleave to the Lord whatever come. If God baffle not the designs of our enemies, they will not rest here, but having begun at the sanctuary, there will be a proceeding to the city; and though ministers may smart first, professors will not want their share. But cleave ye to the Lord, to the purity of doctrine, worship, discipline and government instituted by himself; and though the laws of men should overturn all these, choose you rather to sit by the house of God, though lying in rubbish, than to embrace that in religion which has no stamp but that of human authority, for he is our Lord, and his orders we must obey on all hazards.

Sermon III.

For whom I have suffered the loss of all things.

Philippians iii. 8.

This is a day in which suffering or sinning is set before many in this church; and though our case is extraordinary, yet our good Lord sends us this in our ordinary, which gives an evidence of a due esteem of Christ, which the saints have.

1. We have in the words, the apostle's lot, which tried his esteem of Christ, by his suffering for him. He had spoken much to the commendation of Christ, but many will give Christ a good word, who will not take a frown, an ill word, or a buffet for his sake; but Paul suffered for him.

We have next what he suffered; the loss of all things. When he says *all*, he excepts nothing which might come in competition with Christ, external good things, yea, and internal also, as in competition with him. We have also the cause of his sufferings; they were for Christ, for the sake of that precious one.

Doctrine. God tries, and the saints give proof of their due esteem of Christ, by their suffering the loss of all things for him, as they are called to it. There are two things aimed at in the text, namely, external good things. Saints suffer the loss of these two ways for Christ: 1. In affection, when they lose the predominant affection to them, Luke xiv. 26; when the heart is so far weaned from them, as they are content to part with them, rather than Christ. This is a suffering, in so far as it is not easy, but opposite to nature to be content to let them go for Christ. 2. In action, when they actually lose them for Christ and his cause, and let them go rather than a good conscience. Sometimes storms arise in the church, so as men must either part with Christ, his way, and his truths, or else let all they have go for his sake.

Next internal good things. The saints suffer the loss of these in point of confidence, when all their confidence is carried off them, and laid on Christ alone. Both of these are aimed at in the text. I will now speak a word to the first, namely, external things. And,

I. I will touch at those things which the saints always suffer the loss of in affection, and often in action, for Christ. They must lay their account,

1. With the loss of their credit, esteem, and reputation. "We are fools," says the apostle, "for Christ's sake." None can be wise to the Lord, who are not content to be the world's fools. None will go to heaven but their reputation will run a risk sometime or other. The worldly wise will look upon them as a company of weak men, and the wicked will be ready to count them madmen. Nay, they may lay their account with their credit getting a jog, even among professors also.

2. The loss of their worldly goods, Heb. x. 34. When Joseph is flying from the temptation, the devil takes hold of the mantle of worldly substance, and they must either leave Christ, or they shall not know how to live in the world.

3. The loss of ease and quiet. Sometimes they sit every one under his vine, each at his own table and fireside, but when persecutions arise they may be hunted as partridges, and not have where to lay their heads.

4. The loss of outward comforts and conveniencies. The saints have often got caves for their houses, been exposed to the want of all things, to hunger, thirst, nakedness, with no certain dwelling-place.

5. The loss of their relations. Husbands dragged from their wives, and wives from their husbands. In such cases they lose liberty, and suffer confinement, imprisonment or banishment. Racks, tortures, and scourges, are inflicted upon them, and these often terminate in the loss of their lives, and even after death their bones are not allowed to rest in their graves. Now let us enquire,

II. What it is to suffer these things for Christ. It is to suffer them for Christ's sake. The saints get pardon, peace, and every blessing from God, for Christ's sake; and they must take stripes and blows from the hands of men. But more of this, when God gives another opportunity.

Sermon IV.

For whom I have suffered the loss of all things.
PHILIPPIANS iii. 8.

THE last Lord's day, I told you several things, with the loss of which the saints might lay their accounts for Christ. There is one thing, which, from experience, we are taught they may lay their account to lose, namely, the countenance and protection of the civil magistrate in their duty. This is in itself a great loss. And seeing God has promised to a church, when he is well pleased with her, "that kings shall be her nursing fathers, and their queens her nursing mothers;" the withdrawing of it must be a sign of the Lord's displeasure. Yea, and if we trace the sins of rulers that bear hard on the people to their first spring, we will find that it is some quarrel that God hath with the people, 2 Sam. xxiv. 1. This should humble us, and stir us up to pray for them, and be dutiful to them, to whom the Lord has said, "ye are gods," in every thing that is not inconsistent with your duty to God himself. But this is a trial to us, whether we will regard God or man most; and the saints will ever prefer the countenance of the Lord, to the countenance of the highest powers on earth; and depend upon his protection alone, when they are deprived of all other.

I told you, likewise, what it is to suffer the loss of any thing for Christ. I said, 1. It is to suffer for Christ's sake. 2. For the truths, the ways, and the cause of Christ. I will now add,

3. It is to suffer upon Christ's call to suffering. We are not to cast ourselves into suffering, even for a good cause, at random. We are not lords of ourselves, and therefore must not throw away our peace, goods, liberty, or life, but when God calls for them, and when that is the case, then all should be at his service. Now God calls us to it, when it is brought to that, to suffer or sin. "We must choose rather to suffer affliction with the people of God, than to enjoy the pleasures of sin, which are but for a season." If people cannot get over the waters of suffering but in the devil's boat, which is always a sieve to sink a good conscience, though it may save men's persons and goods, they must even be content to swim. If the cross lie just in the way of duty, and there be no way of getting by it, but by going out of the way, we must even take it up and be going.

4. To suffer for the love of Christ. "Many waters cannot quench love, neither can the floods drown it." This is more than merely to suffer for his sake. Many a man, in time of the church's trouble, gets a blow for Christ's sake, that deserves it not at the enemy's hand; for, at the bottom, they are even men of their own party, the seed of the serpent, though found among Christ's doves; mere hypocrites, they suffer not for Christ, seeing it is not for love to him, of which they are void. A Roman spirit may outbrave death itself; a rugged, opposing spirit may put men to suffer the hardest things, rather than yield. Yea, self is such a salamander as can live in fire, for a good cause. Though we give our bodies to be burned, and have not charity, it profiteth us nothing. But the hearts of honest sufferers are hardened against opposition of men, by soft love to the Lord himself; to his work, cause, and truths, for his own sake. "Thou, Lord, hast given a banner to them that fear thee, that it may be displayed because of the truth."

Lastly, It is to suffer as a member of the body of Christ. "If any man suffer as a Christian, let him not be ashamed; but let him glorify God on this behalf." There was a measure of sufferings laid out for Christ personal, and he alone did bear them: "He endured the cross." But there is a measure of sufferings for Christ mystical, which is divided amongst the members of Christ, as their head sees meet, and every one must take their share; and thus "fill up that which is behind of the afflictions of Christ in their flesh; for his body's sake, which is the church." Some must give in of their goods, some their liberty, some their blood, to fill up this measure. And thus they suffer, that suffer for Christ. I come now to the

III. Thing, Why the Lord trysts his people with suffering the loss of all things for him.

1. Because there are no things which they can long guide well, and he will not permit them to destroy themselves with them. The father gives his child a knife in the sheath, to divert himself with it; but within a little, the child draws out the knife, and plays with it. "Go," says the father, "take it from him, for he will hurt himself with it." So God gives his people ease, peace, and wealth; and so long as these are swallowed up with them in the love of God, they can do them no harm; but alas! they often childishly throw aside the love of the Lord, and solace themselves with the bare worldly enjoyments, and love to these things gets uppermost in their hearts; then comes the word from the Lord, Take them from them. Such a man has made a pillow of security of such a thing, he is sleeping upon it, and minds not his work: go, draw the pillow from under his head, that he sleep not to death upon it. It is no wonder to see wasters want. We have bad long peace in the enjoyment of ordinances. God removes that peace, that he may make us thankful of the crumbs which sometimes fall from our tables. Then the word of the Lord becomes precious, when there is no open vision.

2. To exercise and quicken their graces, to make them thrive the better inwardly. "By this, therefore, shall the iniquity of Jacob be purged; and this is all the fruit, to take away their sin." The Christian, like the palm-tree, or camomile bed, the more he is afflicted, the more he grows. The fire burns hottest in a cold frost, and the wind of persecution makes grace to flame, and blows away the ashes. The waters of affliction cast on the faces of fainting Christians has often made them recover. And sure this generation needs such an awakening. Sufferings tend to the conviction of men, Jer. ii. 23, 35. Solomon tells us, "that oppression maketh a wise man mad;" and a greater than he lets us see it will make a mad man wise, as in the case of the prodigal, Luke xv. 17. No doubt, sufferings will make all of us see faults in our way, which we had no will to acknowledge in our prosperity. Sufferings also make sin bitter. "Thine own wickedness shall correct thee, and thy backslidings shall reprove thee; know therefore, and see, that it is an evil thing and bitter, that thou hast forsaken the Lord thy God." Sin is like Ezekiel's roll, sweet in the mouth, but bitter in the belly. When the Lord writes the sin in the punishment, the smart of the wound will make sin bitter. It will then be as gall and wormwood on the breasts, to wean the child. They are also a hedge in the sinner's way, Hosea ii. 6. Many are riding post away from the Lord, till the cross meet them, as the angel did Balaam, and makes them stand. And truly, if the Lord did not so with us, where would we be in a little time. It is God's goodness to the Church of Scotland, that he doth not allow her to have a long time in sinning, but takes her quickly, when she is going away from him. Afflictions also stir up the saints to take hold of a departing God, Hos. ii. 7. Sufferings are the devil's wedges, driven to separate the saints from Christ. But God makes them cords to draw them to him, and make them cleave to him with purpose of heart, as the child

cleaves to the nurse the more that one offers to pluck it from her.

3. To learn them to live by faith. "I will also leave in the midst of thee an afflicted and poor people, and they shall trust in the name of the Lord." There is never so much glory given to God in believing, as in a suffering time; the promises of the covenant never smell so sweet as then. Nay, there are many promises in the Bible, of which the saints never taste the sweetness till then. While their worldly enjoyments stand entire about them, they live much by sense. While they live at ease in their own houses, the shelter that is in that promise, "Lord, thou hast been our dwelling-place in all ages," is not so sweet as when they have nothing else to depend upon. The daily bread in the promise is not so sweet when we have plenty, as when we are in needy circumstances.

4. To be a real testimony before the world of the superlative excellency of Christ, and the reality of religion. While the world sees men whom they cannot deny to be otherwise wise and sober, and having a due concern about their worldly enjoyments, yet suffer the loss of all, rather than part with Christ and his way, it must needs leave a conviction on their consciences of these things. While they see this, it is a testimony before them to this, that Christ's favour, and way, are better than all the world; preferable to relations, goods, yea, and life itself. For his favour with them weighs down the world's frowns; and the testimony of their conscience, that bird within their breast, makes the sweetest of all melody. This conduct of the saints under sufferings is also a testimony to the life to come against an atheistical generation. What do they fear, that they choose suffering rather than sinning; not the wrath of him "that can only kill the body," for sinning were the way to preserve it; but the wrath of him "that can destroy both soul and body in hell." What do they hope for, great

things in the world? No, they lose what they have, they therefore look for a reward and recompense in another world. It is also a testimony to the power which there is in religion, to wean the heart from the world. "Job is but a dissembler," says the devil, "but put forth thine hand now, and touch all that he hath, and he will curse thee to thy face." But Job makes the devil a liar. There is a power in religion, which makes them suffer the loss of all. It in like manner establishes this grand truth, that there is a power in religion to make men live without these things, which the carnal world cannot want; that there is a communication betwixt God and the soul, that can supply the want of all things. God will let his people see he can make them live very well without these things, and he will let the world see it too, John xiv. 19.

5. It is to make them long for heaven, and so to prepare them for a place among them that stand at his right hand. If they were not so harshly entertained in the world, they would not so much long to be home. But the rugged way which they find in the wilderness makes them long to see the land of Canaan. While the sea of this world is calm to the people of God, they are in hazard of saying, "It is good for us to be here." Therefore the Lord raiseth a storm, the ship is tossed to and fro, then they long to be on shore in Immanuel's land.

6. That what they get, they may the better see from what a blessed hand it comes. God loves to have his people know that they are in his common for what they have in a world. When men have all at hand, they do not so well understand their holding; therefore he calls in his own benefits sometimes, to keep them from hand to mouth; and make them many errands to the throne of grace, that what they had before in a more ordinary way, may come to them as an answer of prayer.

USE 1. Of information. It lets us see,

1. That no man is a saint indeed, but he to whom Christ is dearer than what is dearest to him in the world,

Luke xiv. 26. Every child of God is a martyr either in action or affection. Grace, when it comes into the heart, so looseth all worldly things at the root, that if ever it come to that, that the man must either lose Christ, or lose all, he will suffer rather the loss of all things.

2. That Christ hath not his due esteem in the heart, where the man can by no means suffer the loss of all for him. The shifting of the cross, by sinning against the Lord, however it may prevail sometimes on the saints, if it be a man's habitual practice, will prove him to be none of his, for it says that the love of the world is predominant in such a person.

USE 2. Of exhortation. Let me exhort you then to be ready to evidence your esteem of Christ, by suffering the loss of all things for him, when he calls you to it. Be not offended at the cross of Christ, but embrace it. And be not choosers of the cross. Some will be willing to part with such a thing for Christ, but there is another they cannot part with. But you must make no reserve. Alas! that this exhortation is so very seasonable. The half hour's silence in the heaven of this Church seems to be at an end. The plough that made such deep furrows on the back of this Church formerly, stands now yoked again; the cords of it, which the Lord cut, are knit again, and how soon the word may be given to drive on, we know not. But if it were once set agoing, it is very like it may make deeper furrows on the back of the Church of Scotland than ever it yet made since her youth, though we hope it shall be loosed sooner. Idolatrous papists and superstitions bigots make furious drivers. "Let us contend for the faith once delivered unto the saints," and cleave to that purity of doctrine, worship, discipline, and government, to which this Church hath by the mercy of God attained; to which she stands engaged by the covenants; and which has been handed down to us, sealed with the blood of many martyrs. "Let us stand fast in the liberty wherewith Christ hath made us free." Let our esteem of Christ, his truths, ways and work, be displayed in our suffering the loss of all things, rather than give up with them.

Motive 1. We will betray Christ's cause, if we shift his cross. And woe be to that man who doth this. It is impossible in the way of God's dispensation laid down in the Scripture, that the church should continue in the world without sufferings. "For we must through much tribulation enter into the kingdom of God. Yea, and all that will live godly in Christ Jesus, shall suffer persecution." Do we think that ever the seed of the woman and the seed of the serpent will be at peace? that ever the ship of the church will get to the haven, without the devil's raising a storm to sink her? Where had Christianity been this day, if the primitive Christians had complied with their pagan persecutors, and refused to suffer? Where had the Protestant religion been, if bloody cruelties could have frightened our ancestors into popery? And where had our Church been this day, if the fining, imprisoning, banishing, executing of the opposers of abjured prelacy, had frightened all into a tame compliance with the course of defection then carried on. So that whosoever shall choose to sin rather than suffer, will for his part give Christ and his work freedom to depart out of our coasts.

2. Consider the danger of apostacy from the good ways of the Lord, because of the cross. "If any man draw back," saith God, "my soul shall have no pleasure in him." This makes men unsavoury salt, withered branches, and ordinarily ends in the candle of their life going out with a stink: either going off in fearful stupidity, or horror. "Hold fast, then, the form of sound words as ye have been taught" for many years, and however you may be afterwards trysted, let it appear that you have not heard nor professed in vain. And though grievous wolves enter among you, let it be seen that you are Christ's sheep that discern his voice, and

that will not refuse even his fire mark, rather than to be marked for another.

3. Consider that whatever Christ shall mark out for his, among the things you have, whenever he has said, give up with it for me, it will not be worth the keeping longer. For what? It will be like the manna, which the people kept until the morning, against the express command of God, which stank and bred worms. The plague of God will be in it, and it will never after do you good. "It is a snare to the man who devoureth that which is holy, and after vows to make inquiry." If Christ shall say, Man, give up with your ease, goods, liberty, life, for me; thou hadst better be harrassed, tossed and stripped of thy substance, than be at ease in thy own house, amidst all thy enjoyments. Nothing in the world can be more to us than what God makes it be. We can get no good of what we have, but what goodness God puts in it. But in this the substance is out of it. An evil conscience will put a sting in it, and either silently or violently suck the sap out of it.

4. What is lost for Christ will be the surest and best laid out thing in your possession. It is good lending to the Lord. You will have his bond for it. "And every one that hath forsaken houses, or brethren, or sisters, or father, or mother, or wife, or children, or lands, for my name's sake, shall receive an hundred-fold, and shall inherit eternal life." See here the interest secured, and that is a very extraordinary interest, an hundred for one. That is peace of conscience, joy in the Holy Ghost, sweet contentment, with any thing that is left, and a blessing in it. A little for present support, served up in the dish of a promise and a particular providence, which you will see as if you saw the face of God; which is an hundred-fold better than any thing lost for him. See also the principal secured, but exchanged into eternal life, in heaven.

Sermon V.

For whom I have suffered the loss of all things.

Philippians iii. 8.

Now, let me urge, by a few motives, that ye be not choosers of the cross, but let all without reserve be at his service.

Motive 1. Absolute resignation of ourselves to the will of the Lord is necessary to evidence our sincerity. There is no reality where there is any reserve, for where Christ has the chief room in the heart, every thing will give place to him, Acts xx. 24. The will must be the first sufferer, if ever a man suffer to purpose. It must be melted down into an universal compliance with the will of God.

2. Christ's standard will never be kept up in the world by a company of men who have any thing with which they cannot part for Christ. Persecution is like a fire, that will burn on and consume, aye and until it meet with something that will not burn. The wicked's malice will not end, till they can go no farther.

3. It is in some sort all one what we suffer for Christ; for in our own strength we cannot acceptably suffer the loss of any thing for him; but in his strength we are able to sustain the greatest loss, and yet say, "we have all, and abound." Peter denied Christ, at the voice of a maid; but when strengthened by his Master's grace, his boldness was so astonishingly great, "that even the rulers took knowledge of him that ho had been with

Jesus." The Lord gives people strength suited to their burden. It is as easy for a strong man to lift a stone weight, as for a child to lift a pound.

4. The small things we lose for Christ, are lost indeed as to divine acceptation, when not willing to part with all for him. He will not be served by halves, nor according to our will, Mal. i. 13; 2 John 8.

Lastly, Christ stood at no loss, as too hard for us. He took the whole cup, and wrung out the dregs of it. What had become of us, had Christ dealt with the Father, as we do with him? No, but he was content to be the Father's servant in all, Psal. xl.

DIRECTIONS 1. Labour to get your hearts loosed from the world. "Love not the world, neither the things of the world. If any man love the world, the love of the Father is not in him." Now if you would be thus loosed from the world, then let your hearts be going out more after heaven. I must put these together, for there is no parting of them. The heart will never give up its hold of the world till it be to fix on heaven. So you must do with your hearts as they do with children, when they offer to take one thing from them, they must do it by putting another thing in their hand. Now if the heart were loosed, worldly things would fall off easily, as ripe fruit from a tree; and the affections set on heaven, fit for suffering, Phil. iii. 18, 19, 20.

2. Strive to get the coal of holy zeal blown up in your spirits. A bird shall as soon fly without wings, as one suffer aright without zeal for God. Zeal is an heat of the affections to Christ, his cause, his truths, and way. It is properly an affection that is betwixt married persons, by which they resent the affronts put upon their yoke-fellow, especially with respect to their chastity. "For I am jealous over you," says Paul, "with godly jealousy," 2 Cor. xi. 2, 3. (Greek,) zealous over you with zeal. And if ever there was a time for this zeal, it is now, when so many are crying, let Zion be defiled, when

they are setting themselves to deal with our mother as with an harlot.

3. Study experimental religion. There is no disputing against sense and feeling. Hence the unlearned, but experienced Christian has stood it out, when the disputers of this world have fallen. Study to keep up the power of godliness, communion with God in duties, and to feel the power of truth upon your hearts. Personal holiness in men's private walk is an excellent help to their keeping right in public trials.

4. Renew your repentance, and let there be no standing quarrel betwixt God and you. Unmortified, unrepented sin, leaves a sting in the conscience, deprives us of confidence with God, and so unfits us for bearing the cross.

Lastly, Live by faith. "The just shall live by faith." Let faith be employed to cast your burden on the Lord; the burden of your duty, protection, provision, and through-bearing on Christ, and to keep in your eye the promised reward, Heb. xi. 26.

I should now come to speak of these things of which the saints suffer the loss, in point of confidence, for Christ. But I have before, on the third verse, spoken of these things, internal and external, with which they give up in point of confidence. I will only hint at two things:

1. The saints suffering the loss of their sufferings for Christ, in point of confidence in them. Sirs, you heard what you may be obliged to lose for Christ; but I will tell you one thing more which you must give up for him, when you have suffered the loss of all these; and that is, all confidence in these your sufferings, or else you will lose them all indeed; as when you have done, so when you have suffered, "you must say you are unprofitable servants." They will perish in their sufferings, who make their sufferings their confidence before the Lord. Consider,

1. This has been the way of all honest sufferers, Gal. vi. 14; compare 2 Cor. xi. 23. See also Rev. vii. 14, 15. When they have lost all for him, they have renounced confidence in all, and fled naked to the horns of the altar, and durst not plead for his favour for their sufferings, but for the Lord's sufferings.

2. To plead upon sufferings for Christ is a dreadful mark of a graceless sufferer, Matth. xx. 12–16. It is a sign men seek themselves and not the Lord in their sufferings, therefore they get their penny, the credit and reputation among the saints that they were seeking, and that is all.

3. What is the Lord obliged to us, when we have suffered the loss of all? Have we done more than our duty; yea, than our interest led us to? If a beggar should come in, and crave his alms as debt, because, forsooth, he stood at your door, and would not go away, though a heavy rain was falling on him all the time, what would you think of his plea? So it is with us, if we plead the merit of our sufferings.

4. None of our sufferings will abide the trial of the law, so that in our best performances that way there is sin to condemn us. So that if God would enter into judgment with us for our sufferings, we would be ruined by them. The greatest patience wants not a mixture of impatience, and the strongest faith some remaining unbelief.

Lastly, It is our honour to suffer for Christ, and considering our unworthiness and sinfulness, we may wonder if ever God honour the like of us to bear his cross. And therefore such persons are deeper in debt to free grace than other persons; because that they had any thing to lose for Christ, which many have not, and that when they had it, they had a heart to part with it for him.

2. I would take notice of the difficulty of parting with these things, in point of confidence. Such a diffi-

culty it was to the apostle, that it was a perfect suffering on his part. He had a difficulty in renouncing them, but yet he did it.

1. It is difficult, for it is above nature to do it. It is harder for a man to renounce confidence in his suffering, than it is to suffer; or in his duties when done, than it is to do them. The latter are not beyond the power of nature, the former are, Phil. iii. 3; Matth. v. 3. The influence of the law may bear a man out to the latter, but gospel grace is necessary to the former.

It is contrary to nature to do it. Not only nature cannot do it, but cannot but resist the doing of it. Nature bends always to the way of the covenant of works, which was to depend upon the good done by the man himself, and is opposite to the way of believing, which carries a man out of himself to Christ. This is a suffering to a proud heart, to have its beautiful feathers thus pulled down and trampled in the dust. To be obliged to another for life, while it thought it had a sufficiency of its own. To be at pains to do and suffer for the Lord, and after all to be obliged to renounce all it has done and suffered, and betake itself to the doing and suffering of another: to work for the winning of heaven, and then to overlook all as if they had done nothing. It is no evidence of acquaintance with the heart, where men find nothing of this difficulty. This weed grows in all men's hearts naturally, however few do sweat at the plucking it up. Amen.

Sermon VI.

And do count them but dung, that I may win Christ.

Philippians iii. 8.

Many are mistaken in their first accounts, and therefore throw away what they would gladly take up again, when they have made a second reckoning. Such are the foolish builders, Luke xiv. 29. But the apostle, who first counted all loss, and then parted with them for Christ, upon a review counts them but dung or dog's meat, such things as are only fit to be cast to the dogs: and so repents not his parting with them, but takes his heart away from them all, that he may gain Christ. This was his grand object in the world, to which all things behoved to yield. And gaining Christ with the loss of all, counts himself a great gainer.

Doctrine I. It is the Christian's grand object in the world, and should be the grand design of every one, to win, or gain Christ.

O, my brethren! what is your grand object or design in the world? what is the great business which you have in view? No doubt it is to win something. But what is that something which you chiefly set yourselves to win? Is it to win preferment? to win an estate? a stock to yourselves, and your families to live upon, after you? To win a livelihood? Are these your grand objects in the world? I fear most of us rise no higher. These are too mean, too grovelling. I shew you a more excellent way. If you make not this your choice, you will be fools indeed.

I. I will shew you what it is to win Christ, and how we are to win him.

II. Give the reasons of the point. Let us then,

I. Shew what it is to win Christ, and how we are to win him.

To win or gain Christ, is to get him to be ours. To get an interest in him, and enjoy him. This we have always to seek till we come to heaven, where we will have the full enjoyment of him. This is that which is the grand object of some, and should be of us all. Now this winning of Christ imports, that naturally we are without Christ, Eph. ii. 12. He is not ours naturally. This spiritual relation to Christ must be by the sinner's consent, who must take him for Lord and Husband, and then he is theirs. But all naturally are destitute of an interest in this blessed treasure. It imports, also, that Christ is gain. They are great gainers that get him. He is an inestimable treasure, "the treasure hid in the field." "The one pearl of great price." They are enriched for ever that have him to be theirs. Lose who will, they are gainers. The blind world see no beauty for which he is to be desired. But it is no wonder to see the most gainful bargain slighted by fools, who have a price put into their hand to get it, but have no heart for it. It imports that this gain may be got. We may have Christ for the winning. The treasure is hid in the field, they may have it that will dig for it. Christ is revealed and offered in the gospel. The door of access to him is open. The proclamation is made, "whosoever will, let him take the water of life freely." It is our own fault if we want him. But they that will have him must win him ere they can get him. People must not think to sit at ease, and wait till heaven drop down into their months; or that an interest in Christ, and the enjoyment of him, will be obtained by drowsy wishes, with folded hands. No, we must lay this bargain to heart, and leave no stone unturned to make it effectual; nay, in order to win him,

1. We must work and win as labourers do. "Work out your own salvation with fear and trembling." It will cost working, and sore working. What severer work, than that of those who dig in mines. "If thou seekest her as silver, and searchest for her as for hid treasures, then shalt thou understand the fear of the Lord, and find the knowledge of God." Up then, you lazy souls, if you would have a Christ; you must put your hand to work; yea, your heart must be set to work. "Ye shall seek me and find, saith the Lord; when you shall search for me with all your heart." God gives Christ freely; but I assure you it is to labourers, not to loiterers, that gift is made. You will toil sore to win something for the body, but what are you doing to win Christ?

2. We must fight and win as soldiers. "The kingdom of heaven suffereth violence, and the violent take it by force." If you have a mind for Christ, to come even to his seat, you must fight your way to it. "To him that overcometh," saith he, "will I give to sit with me on my throne; even as I also overcame, and as set down with my Father in his throne." Whenever a soul is on the way to Christ, the alarm is sounded in hell, and if the soul will have him, it must have him in opposition to flesh and blood, principalities and powers. You must fight your way through the white band of the world's smiles, profits, and pleasures; and refuse to be held by these silken cords, which the devil uses to keep souls from Christ; and also through the black band of temptations, doubts, fears, discouragements, that he will muster up against you; and, by all appearance, the red band too, so that it may cost you to resist unto blood, Heb. xii. 4. Sometimes Satan gets plunderings, prisons, tortures, yea, and death, set up between Christ and them that would be at him; but you must fight and win, saying,

in all these things, "we shall be more than conquerors, through him that loved us."

3. We must wrestle and win, as those do who strive for the mastery, Eph. vi. 12–14. There will be a combat, in which you must be engaged against your own lusts, "for the flesh lusteth against the Spirit, and the Spirit against the flesh." If you tamely yield, truly you will never win Christ. You must in his strength cast them down, get them nailed to his cross, and make your way over them, to the enjoyment of himself. You must cut off right hands, and pluck out right eyes, that you may win Christ.

4. We must run and win as racers do. "So run that ye may obtain." "Lay aside every weight, and the sin that doth most easily beset you, and run with patience the race set before you." There is a race proposed by the Lord, namely, the profession of the truth, and practice of holiness. The Lord Christ and his apostles opened the race, and ever since that time there have been many who engaged to run that race. But as soon as it was opened, the devil planted thorns on the race ground, kindled fires, set up gibbets, laid misery, shame, grief, poverty, and temptations of all sorts in the way. Many fell, many turned back, a great many run faintly, but all go forward that win Christ. In the world, men suppose but two fixed points, the highest and the lowest; the bodies betwixt the two are in continual motion. In the rational world, the glorified are in the highest point, the damned in the lowest. Both fixed, neither of them can go farther. We that are betwixt the two, are in motion either to heaven or hell. If we would win Christ, then, let us set our face heavenward, and run and win.

5. We must trade and win as merchants do. "The kingdom of heaven is like unto a merchantman seeking goodly pearls; who, when he had found one pearl of great price, went and sold all that he had, and bought it." And, as spiritual merchants, we must be at pains;

we must exchange and win, as they do. They that have a mind for Christ, have much business in the royal exchange of heaven. And you will say they win indeed, if you consider what they exchange with the Lord. "A new heart also," says he, "will I give you, and a new spirit will I put within you; and I will take away the stony heart out of your flesh, and will give you a heart of flesh." Christ takes off their rags, and gives them his robes of righteousness. He frees them from the curse, and sends them away with the blessing. You must also sell and win, as merchants do. I had occasion, on another subject, to tell you how you must sell all you have at the market of free grace, Mark x. 22, and condescended on the particulars which you are to sell. Be sure this is a gaining trade.

You must also buy and win, as merchants do. I find three things, which the spiritual merchant, who would win Christ, is this day called to buy. Precious truth. "Buy the truth, and sell it not." It can never be too dear bought; whatever people may pay for it, they are gainers. This is like to be a time for selling of the truth, and persons of Judas' trade will never be wanting, saying, "what will you give me, and I will deliver him unto you." But let men get for it what they will, they will find at length that they have made a fool's bargain, and they will be losers at the end of the day. "For what is a man profited, if he shall gain the whole world, and lose his own soul? Or what shall a man give in exchange for his soul?" A second thing you ought to buy, is precious time. "Redeeming the time," says Paul. We have had a long time of selling it, and squandering it away, though we have not enriched ourselves with the price. We have allowed our precious opportunities of communion with God to go for trifles. But buy again now, for the days are evil. That is, as the merchant who has foolishly neglected his business most of the day, plys it most eagerly when he sees the market is near a close, if by any means he may make up his former loss. So do you. The third thing you must buy, is the precious riches of Christ. "I counsel thee," says he, "to buy of me gold tried in the fire, that you may be rich; and white raiment, that you may be clothed." His merit; that is, gold able to purchase heaven. His righteousness; raiment for your souls. His Spirit; salve for your blind eyes. It is a blessed market this. You cannot but be gainers. Here we are to "buy without money and without price." For I hope you will not count upon renouncing your own merits, righteousness and wisdom, as a price for these things. You must also export and import, as merchants do. Our trade to heaven consists much in our export to Immanuel's land. And what have we to export, but the home product of guilt, weakness, poverty and wants. But let us carry them all away to the Lord, we will gain by it, leaving them there. We must import the products of the King's country, consisting of pardons for our guilt, strength for our weakness, and fulness for our wants, and then we will gain indeed. We now proceed,

II. To give reasons of the point. It is the Christian's great object to win Christ, and should be the great object of all.

1. Because if we win Christ, we gain all. This is the shortest way to make up a stock, a treasure that will enrich us for ever, in time and eternity. He thought so who said, "one thing have I desired of the Lord; that will I seek after." So also did the wise merchant, Matth. xiii. 45, 46. He were a foolish man who would spend his time in making a great number of petty bargains, by which he gained but little, and would neglect a bargain that would make up for all his days, when in his offer. Thou art the man, whose great object is not to win Christ. If you win Christ, you are made up for time. "Godliness is profitable unto all things, having the promise of the life that now is." What would you have for time? Would you have food and raiment? win

Christ, and you shall have them. With the kingdom of God your great object, "all these things shall be added unto you." It will be a very bad time indeed, in which Christ's spouse may not promise herself food and raiment. It is not an uncertain, but sure thing: "Bread shall be given her, her water shall be sure." She wants then only a dwelling-place: well, "she shall dwell on high; yea, the Lord himself is her dwelling-place, in all generations." But some people would have land too. Then there is no such sure way to make a purchase as this, win Christ. He is Lord of all the land in the world, and the whole earth is thine in the right of thy husband, Matth. v. 5. But what will people do for money? Win Christ, and you shall not want it. "The Almighty shall be thy defence, and thou shalt have plenty of silver." (Hebrew,) gold; and the silver of thy strength.

Objection. Yes, says the unbeliever, these are brave words, but depend upon them, and see what they will bring in to thy treasure, Answer. They are God's words, and his good words are better than all the world's good deeds. God gives some persons, for whom he hath no special care, their portion in their hand, and sends them away; and others, his dearest children, he gives them the good words of a promise, and keeps them at home with himself. Say now, who has the best of it, Matth. xxv. 34, "Ye blessed of my Father;" (Greek,) you to whom my Father hath spoken well. God's good words have always good deeds in their bosom. He will not approve of those who say to the needy, "be ye clothed, be ye fed, but give not the things that are needful for the body." And will he be found such an one himself? No, no. Many of the saints have depended upon his words, and they have been fed and clothed, and left their experience on record, Psal. xxxiv. 6–10. They have declared, that like the disciples, "they had lacked nothing." The mistake of the unbeliever is, he thinks God's bond cannot be paid, unless it be paid in cash, the very thing itself. No, God can make it out another way, and his people can say, "as having nothing, and yet possessing all things." Had Moses any reason to complain, when he wanted meat forty days, when God so supported him, that he needed it not. Adam lived very well at first, when the heaven was the roof of his house, the earth his floor, the grass his seat, and the shade of trees his bed-chamber. He did not complain of the want of a house, when God was his God, and he was so provided. Stamped leather has sometimes gone for money, and they that had enough of it were even as rich as they that have the silver and gold now; and if it was as good, I hope you may allow the Almighty himself to be better than gold.

Again, thou art made up for eternity. "Godliness is profitable unto all things, having the promise of the life that now is, and of that which is to come." Come death when it will, thy lodging is taken up on the other side of Jordan. Thou hast won the Lord of the land to be thine, how canst thou be but welcome there? John xiv. 2. The law cannot lay aught to thy charge, for he has satisfied it, and thou mayest say, "I am crucified with Christ, nevertheless I live." Justice cannot apprehend thee, for the debt is paid and Christ has got up thy discharge. When the gain of other people, who are winning the world, is at an end, thy gain is but in some sort beginning to come in, but it is a gain that will tell out through the ages of eternity.

2. Because if we win not Christ, we win nothing, we lose all. We lose our souls, and where is our gain then? Matth. xvi. 26. Without Christ, without hope, for he is the only way to the Father, John xiv. 6. The wise people of the world need not boast of their winning; they are penny wise and pound foolish, win what they will, seeing they win not Christ. Whatever they are winning, there is a thousand times more going to destruction in the meantime. Would he be a wise man that would go

abroad in the harvest, and while he is winning by some little bargain, his whole crop in the meantime is shaken with the wind, and rotten with the rain. That is thy case, O man! thou art abroad winning the world, but all is going wrong at home within thy own soul. And when thou comest home to thyself, at death, or otherwise, it will be sad. Whatever you are winning, is but like children winning of their fellows, that will never make them rich, never buy meat nor clothes to them. It is money "for that which is not bread, and labour for that which satisfieth not." A thousand worlds will not purchase a pardon; a heaven to you, without which you will be miserable. It is a poor trade, where a man is not winning Christ. It will never bring him the one thing necessary, and what winning can be there?

Whatever you are winning, if you would count what you give out, as well as what you get in, you would find all your winning is worse than nothing. Count your days, your precious time, precious opportunities of grace and salvation, your precious souls laid out in winning the things of the world, but not Christ; each of which is far more precious than what you can win that way, and you will see you win nothing by the bargain, but are great losers.

USE 1. It reproves several sorts of persons; and first, those who are taken up about nothing but to win the world, utterly neglecting to win Christ, and to get an interest in him. There is little difference between such and the brutes. They work, and eat, and sleep; these are the all of the beasts, and the all of some who are worse than the beasts. They never seriously set themselves to get matters right for their souls. It were their advantage that they could die as the beasts, as they live like them.

You whose business it is to win Christ, but it is not your main business. It is but a bye-hand work with you. It is the world that is nearer your hearts than an interest in Christ, and the enjoyment of him. You walk with

God at all adventures. Assure yourselves that no man will stumble upon Christ by accident, or snapper into heaven, or fall into it by guess. If you make it not your chief business, you may gain a name, but you will never win Christ.

Those who sell the truth and a good conscience, that they may get the world kept. People that will sail with every wind, and keep always on the side that is upmost in the world, are not in the way to win Christ; "For we can do nothing against the truth, but for the truth." Take heed to yourselves, our time is like to be an ensnaring time. You will be fair to lose the world and its countenance, or to lose Christ. But be you ready to let all go which you cannot hold in his own way, with his favour.

Those who will not stand to sell soul and conscience, to win something of the world, if they can but get their hands on it. They are careful for nothing but their credit, which is in hazard too, if so be they can gain some little thing in the world. It seems we have such persons among us, by the frequent complaints people are making of their losses that way, not only by picking, but stealing. May the good Lord discover them for a terror to others! O! how are people's consciences thus seared, and their hearts hardened to defy that curse, that roll of curses that God has said he will send into the house of the thief, Zech. v. 4; that bill of eternal exclusion from heaven, passed against the unrighteous, 1 Cor. vi. 9, 10. Read their doom, Deut. xxix. 19, 20.

USE 2. I exhort you to make it your main business in the world to win Christ. Consider this is the way in which every person may win, the poor as well as the rich. It is not much the most part of us can rationally propose to win to ourselves in the world. It is difficult to win much, unless people have a good stock, and be very diligent also. But come here and win, even you that hath no money.

You have been at pains to win something of the world. Some of you have won, some of you have lost; many of you have real difficulty to win your daily bread. You have tried the one, will you not do so much as try the other also. Sirs, if you will not, your toil, sweat, and weariness, in winning the world, will be a witness against you before the Lord, that you could be at pains for other things, but at no pains for Christ.

This is the shortest way of winning. No man will choose the winning by many small bargains, when he can win all that and more by one great bargain. This is the case, win Christ and you win all. In short, it is a safe and sure way of winning. The best traders that ever carried on merchandise have lost of some bargains; but never one was a loser here. You will be sure to win if you set yourself to win Christ, and your winning will be beyond your expectation.

Lastly, It is a durable winning that can never be lost. People will be winners one year, and lose all that and more, another year; win of one bargain, and lose it again of another: but win Christ once, and you will never again lose your winning.

Use. 3. Of trial. You may see whether you be Christians or not. Try what is your grand object. Is it to win Christ, or not? You may know it by what follows.

Doctrine. II. They whose grand object in the world is to wia Christ, will count all but dung that comes in competition with this bargain. For explication of this, they will count,

1. Nothing too much for him, but be content to have Christ on any terms. They will say, "Lord, what wilt thou have me to do." Dung is a worthless thing, that nobody makes account of. They will think no pains too much for him; and they that think otherwise, never saw the worth of the pearl, Prov. ii. 4, 5. They will hang on about his door, and think they speed well, if

they be heard at length. They will count no cost too much. Sometimes men have a cheap religion; but it is not to be supposed that they will always get the Lord served with that which cost them nothing. It is very like that God will have a costly sacrifice of the hand of these nations; to which both his own people, and the enemies of religion and of his work, shall be obliged to contribute both of their goods and of their blood. These lands are defiled with blood. So many murderers escaping unpunished; and the blood of the saints shed in these nations remains unpurged, though it is like there may be more put to it, and the land may get blood to drink. It nearly concerns us that God hath said, "I will bring a sword upon you, that shall avenge the quarrel of my covenant." We have mixed with the nations and learned of them their ways, and justly may the Lord send the instruments of his vengeance from the places from which we have brought the atheism and profanity of the day. But cost what it will, the saints will think nothing too much, so as they win Christ.

2. Cost what it will, they will not think that they are even hands, but that they are gainers, if they can win Christ. Whatever be laid in the balance with Christ, it is but so much dung and dross for so much gold. They must lay out for Christ, lusts dear as right eyes; yea, it may be also goods, liberty, and life. The carnal world cannot see how they can hold their own with such trading, and therefore will trade no such way. But he whose grand object is to win Christ, considers it the most gainful bargain; even a hundred-fold got in, for one given out, Matth. xix. 29.

3. Have what they will, they will count they have nothing, while they have not Christ. What avail barns, and coffers full of dung, to a man? What do food and clothing, riches and honour, avail to a man who sees the need and the worth of Christ? Will he not be ready to say, what wilt thou give me, if I go Christless? These

things can do no more to my poor soul, than dung to my body. Could the soul dwell and feed with the swine, they would have enough, while they have dog's meat. This says, few make it their grand object to win Christ, seeing so many can live and reign as kings without him; and give them the world and their lusts, and they have the desire of their hearts.

4. Win what they will, they will count they win nothing, if they win not Christ. It is but dung they can win that way. The world thinks godly people fools, while they care not for winning, as they do. But see the world's fool's, while they lose so egregiously, yet count themselves gainers. Achan was no gainer, when he brought into his tent a wedge of gold, and a weight of wrath far heavier than the wedge. That meat is but dog's meat, that has a bone in it to stick in the throat of the eater. The open fields are better than a house in which brimstone is scattered on the habitation. Wealth, with the want of God's favour, is but dung in comparison of want, with God's good will. I am afraid there are but few who count this way.

5. Be about them what will, if Christ be not in them, they will count themselves loathsome with it all, like persons that have nothing but dung about them, Job ix. 31; therefore they count wicked men vile men, Psal. xv. 4. Rags, with righteousness, are more desirable to them than robes and gay apparel, where there is a naked soul. What is a throne for the body but dung, while Christ has not the throne of the heart; or riches, while men are not rich toward God.

6. Be in their way what will, to hinder them from Christ, they will shovel it out of their way as dung, rather than be kept back from Christ, Song viii. 6. 7. Him they cannot want, him they must have. "Cast ye up, cast ye up, prepare the way; take up the stumbling-block out of the way of my people." They must be at Zion; and if they should cut their way through rocks and over

mountains, they must be there; if a Red Sea were before them, it shall not stop them. O! how easily are the most of us kept back from Christ! Little thing will stand betwixt him and us, which we will be as loathe to cast out of our way, as if it were gold.

Lastly, If they cannot shovel it out of their way, they will tread and trample on it as dung, that they may win Christ. "Thus Levi said unto his father, and to his mother, I have not seen him; neither did he acknowledge his brethren, nor knew his own children; for they have observed thy word, and kept thy covenant." The street of the New Jerusalem is laid with gold, for the citizens thereof will tread on gold, and on what is most valuable in the world, that they may get forward to God. If waters be in their way, they will pass through them; and if fires, they will walk over them, and therefore all the travellers to Zion "have their feet shod with the preparation of the gospel of peace."

USE 1. Of information. This lets us see that there are few in the world whose grand object is to win Christ; so far are they from counting that dung which comes in competition with Christ. Nay, instead of that, people are worshipping dung gods, so the original calls idols. The gods of many are no other than gods coming out of the earth. It is the earth, and what is in it, that has most of their hearts. The belly is the god of many, the world of others, for covetousness is idolatry; yea, who is the god of this world, but the devil, Beelzebub; that is, the god of dung, (Syriac.)

They are also wallowing in the mire of profanity, 2 Pet. ii. 22. Mire, the word properly signifies the dung that is carried out of stables in which swine wallow. And what are these profane courses, but that which comes out of the vile stable of an unrenewed heart, Mark vii. 21. And alas! many washed swine are found there, who sometimes appeared another thing than they are now.

They are loading themselves with the thick clay of the world, Hab. ii. 6. Taking a complete burden of the world, pressing them so that they cannot get up their heads toward heaven. Surely these count not the world dung, or less of it would serve them. The cares of it stretch their minds like tenter hooks, and are Satan's cords binding them down to the earth, that they cannot lift up their souls to the Lord. Thus the houses of many are but dunghills, where all is for the world, nothing for God and themselves, but dung to fatten the earth, not to help to replenish heaven. Dust is their meat, for they are the serpent's seed, Isaiah lxv. 25. That is to say, they fetch their satisfaction from their lusts, they cannot rejoice in God, nor in the ways of holiness. These things are tasteless to them, and nothing relishes with them, but the husks of sin, which the swine of the world eat.

Finally, The worship of many is but dung and loathsome. God says to the in, "I will spread dung on your faces, even the dung of your solemn feasts." There is nothing of spirit in their worship. It is but a loathsome carcase of bodily exercise, which is good for nothing but to be cast out. They may value it themselves, for sometimes dung was valued highly, when "a fourth part of a cab of it was sold for five pieces of silver," but God abhors it. There was a gate in Jerusalem called the dung-gate, Neh. ii. 13. Such may be in the church, but they will be carried out at the dung-port by death, or otherwise; and see their end, "they shall perish forever, like their own dung; they who have seen them shall say, where are they?"

Use 2. Evidence yourselves true Christians, by counting thus. There are three parts of counting, which the carnal world cannot learn, but Christians learn them at the school of Christ:

1. Counting days. "So teach us," says Moses, "to number our days, that we may apply our hearts to wisdom." The carnal, when they begin to count their time,

they number by years, and many years, Luke xii. 19; and hence they always fool away the present time. But the Christian will count by days, and these few days short and uncertain, Gen. xlvii. 9; and "so apply their hearts unto wisdom."

2. Counting afflictions and trials to be gainful. The carnal world can make nothing of these that is desirable, but the total of them is still grief, sorrow, and loss; they cannot see how to make more of them. But the godly are taught to count them light, momentary, and gainful; yea, "as working for them a far more exceeding and eternal weight of glory." They count them all joy, and that they are happy that endure them, James i. 2, and v. 11.

3. Counting things of this world, in competition with Christ, to their true value. The world is ever completely wrong in this counting. Here they count their mites to talents; and instead of fifty, set down an hundred. They count them ever above their worth, better than Christ and his favour. But Christians have learned to count them at another rate, all loss and dung for Christ; and I would have you count so. Consider,

1. How God accounts of them. The verdict of the Spirit concerning all is, "vanity of vanity, all is vanity." "Riches are that which is not." Agrippa's great pomp is, in the language of the Holy Ghost, much fancy, (Greek,) Acts xxv. 23. God is no accepter of persons. None of these tilings commend us to God, more than if we were naked and bare; the judgment of God is according to truth. Consider,

2. How you will account of them when you are going into another world, and when you are there. When death stares you in the face, and gives you a warning away from all you possess, what will you think of them then? When you are in another world, and standing before the judgment-seat of Christ, whether will grace or

gold, robes or righteousness, Christ or the world, be of greatest value in your eyes?

3. Consider you will never honour Christ, and if so, he will never honour you. You will never honour him in your hearts, while you prefer every thing to him; nor in your lives, by doing much, or suffering for his cause. A man that counts not thus, is not fit for such a time as this, in which God seems to be about to put it to the trial, what men think of the world, in comparison of Christ.

Labour then to get a view of the glory, riches, and excellency of Christ, and then you will count all things but dung for him. If men knew the worth of Christ, they would think nothing too much for him.

DOCTRINE III. They are truly winners, lose what they will, that gain Christ. To confirm this point, consider,

What he is in himself. He is God, and so if he be yours, God is yours, for he is God; the Son of God begotten by the Father, by an eternal unspeakable generation, so that he has life in himself. He is man, God-man, fairer than the children of men. The human nature is united to the divine in the person of the Son, and so lies at the fountain head, as the bowl in Zechariah's candlestick.

2. Consider what he is to us:

1. Winning Christ, we gain a ransom for our souls. "He gave himself for us, to redeem us from all iniquity." If one were a slave to the Turks, what matter what he lost, if he gained a ransom for himself. We are debtors to justice, criminals in law, prisoners of Satan, bound over to the wrath of God by nature. Now the soul's redemption is precious. If we could gain the whole world, that could not ransom us, Hos. xiii. 14; Job xxxiii. 24.

2. Winning Christ, we gain a purchase. He not only ransoms us from the wrath of God, but purchaseth heaven to us. He gives us gold tried in the fire, to enrich

us. If Christ be thine, he communicates his merit to thee for thy justification, and title to eternal life; so that it is a righteous thing for thee to get heaven, 2 Thess. i. 6, 7.

3. Winning Christ, we gain a treasure; the treasure hid in the field. Consider that whatever you can lose for Christ, if you win him, you win a treasure, when you lose but some small mite for it. Christ is a treasure for preciousness, everything in Christ is precious. When Solomon counted all that was in the world, he sets down the total in two great cyphers, vanity and vexation. And is this the prize for our sweat and cares? Why so eager on vanity, so fond of vexation. But all in Christ is precious. Is not grace, pardon, peace, precious? They were purchased with his precious blood, 1 Pet. i. 19; they are wrapped up in precious promises, 2 Pet. i. 4. O precious promises! where happiness is wrapt up in words and syllables. Eternity couched in a sentence! an eternal weight of glory in a word! Christ is also a treasure, for variety and abundance of precious things. The treasure of worldly things is soon counted. We have the inventory of it, consisting but of these three things, "the lust of the eye, the lust of the flesh, and the pride of life." But it "hath pleased the Father, that in Christ should all fulness dwell." "Eye hath not seen, nor ear heard, neither hath it entered into the heart of man to conceive, the things which God hath laid up for them that love him." I will only tell you of the following things in it. The whole constellation of graces, each more precious than gold, of more worth than a world. The whole privileges of the saints: an eternal weight of glory. *Finally*, the whole Trinity. Christ is also a treasure in respect of secrecy. Hid to the unrenewed world, and even to believers in a great measure. "It doth not yet appear what we shall be; but we know that, when he shall appear, we shall be like him; for we shall see him as he is." But even in glory, they will never see to the end of it.

4. Winning Christ, we gain that which will turn every thing to our advantage. "All things shall work together for our good." This is the stone that turns all to gold. If we be in Christ, death shall be profitable to us as an inlet to eternal bliss; the grave, a place of rest, as God's field, where the seed sown shall spring up with increase; the wind of afflictions shall drive us more speedily to our harbour; our crosses shall be for crucifying our lusts; our losses shall be our gain to bring an hundred-fold. Thus, in a word, all things shall work for our good.

5. Winning Christ, we gain an heirship. We "become heirs of God, and joint heirs with Christ." More by far, than if we were heirs of the greatest monarch on earth. By this you will be heirs of the promises, young heirs of glory. Attended by angels, and duly provided for while in your minority, and at length admitted to your inheritance. Yea, all is yours.

6. There is nothing, then, which we have to lose for Christ, that is worthy to be laid in the balance with him. The loss is infinitely made up in him. What are our worldly goods, in comparison of the goodness laid up for those that are in Christ. May not the relation to Christ and his Father make up all the loss of other relations? The glorious liberty of the sons of God, make up the loss of our liberty in the world; and an eternal life, our natural life.

Lastly, It is below the honour of God to let sinners be losers at his hand. He will not be behind with his creatures. They shall have good measure, pressed down and running over. "But now they desire a better country, that is, an heavenly; wherefore God is not ashamed to be called their God, for he hath prepared for them a city."

USE 1. Of information. The worldly man is penny wise and pound foolish. "He strains at a guat and swallows a camel." He will be loath to lose a sixpence, but he can let a talent of glory slip through his fingers. He watcheth a little gilded earth, lays it up securely, holds it fast in his hand, nay, in his heart; but he can let a crown, a kingdom, a heaven, a Christ go. Though it is difficult to beguile him in other things, he will be cheated out of these for a trifle, like a child. Esau was a cunning man, yet he was as easily cheated of the blessing as if he had been a fool or idiot.

2. In a time of giving out for Christ, they are not the greatest gainers that lose nothing for him. When the trial is over, and every one counts their winning, the greatest losers will be found the greatest gainers. The greatest outgiving has the greatest income, as in the parable of the talents. Alas! what is the winning of others, but that they have saved the shoe, but lost the foot; saved the cabinet, but lost the jewel; saved the body, but lost the soul; the world is gained, Christ is lost.

Use 2. Of exhortation. "Buy the truth, and sell it not." Win Christ at any rate, lose him at no rate. Remember you cannot make too dear a purchase in this point. There are three cases in which I would have you to walk by this principle,

1. When sin comes to you, like Potiphar's wife to Joseph, and offers you deadly poison in a golden dish. Now Christ and a lust are in competition. Now here is a goodly price offered you for the Lord's favour and countenance; but sell it not, for all you can make by it will not clear the cost, but it will be bitterness in the end. Now you must have him at the rate of plucking out a right eye, yet buy the truth, assure yourself it is cheap enough of all.

2. When sloth comes to you, as Peter to Christ, covering a sharp sword with words softer than oil, saying, "Master, spare thyself," what needs all this trouble about religion? What needs such bitter repenting, wrestling in prayer, watching over heart and life? What needs this exposing yourself for a sermon? Now sloth

and Christ are come in competition. Here is a goodly price for Christ, a sound sleep on the sinner's soft bed, a way strewed with roses, pleasant carnal company, and a warm fireside; but sell it not so cheap: all that is not worth one smile of his face: nay, of one check from him. Take him, though at the rate of the most exquisite diligence, the most painful exercise, most difficult and grating to the flesh, and cheap enough.

3. When the enemies of Christ and his work come to you, as the chief priests to Judas, offering you thirty pieces if you will betray him; and when you are put to loss in his cause, say, like Judas to the honest woman that bestowed a box of ointment on Christ, "What needs all this waste?" Now Christ and the world are in competition. Here is a goodly price for Christ. You may keep what you have, and also get more; you shall get the world's smiles, if you will venture on his frowns. Let them guide God's house as they will, and you shall dwell in ceiled houses. Take the mark of the beast in your foreheads, or in your hands, and you shall obtain leave to buy and sell. But sell him not. The world's offer is not worth the hearing; it is but dung for gold, counters for pearls. But in such a case you cannot have him, but at the expense of the world's countenance, loss of means, and perhaps liberty and life itself, but he cannot be too dear bought.

Motive. You will get all in Christ that you are seeking to win in the world, and more. If you would have a name, you shall get one, better than that of sons and daughters. Would you have honour? you shall have it. "Him that honoureth me," says God, "I will honour." Would you have gold? you shall have it. The very streets of heaven are paved with gold. Amen.

Sermon VII.

And be found in him.

Philippians iii. 9.

Here is another thing which the apostle hath in his eye, namely, to be found in Christ. This supposeth that they who win Christ are in him, united to him, and that they who are united to him will be found in him, when God searcheth for them. Having before handled the doctrine of union with Christ, I shall only speak to this.

Doctrine. It should be men's great care, to provide that when God comes to search, they may be found in Christ. Here I shall,

I. Shew how, or when God comes to search, and the saints are found in Christ.

II. How and where they shall be found, that are found in Christ.

III. Give the reasons of the point, and then subjoin some improvement. I am then,

I. To shew how or when God comes to search, and the saints are found in Christ. This world is a confused heap, and many times the counterfeits are found among the jewels, undiscerned; but God hath searching times, in which he will search out men. "I will," says he, "search Jerusalem with candles, and punish the men that are settled in their lees, that say in their heart, The Lord will not do good, neither will he do evil."

1. One searching time is, a time of plain searching, preaching of the word. The word is God's candle, which he kindles to let men see through their state and condition. "The word of God is quick and powerful, sharper than any two-edged sword, piercing even to the dividing asunder of soul and spirit, and of the joints and marrow, and is a discerner of the thoughts and intents of the heart." God carries this candle through the man's spirit, and searcheth him thoroughly. Thus Paul tells us, that by such searching preaching "even an unbeliever, or unlearned man, is convinced of all, he is judged of all; and thus are the secrets of his heart made manifest; and so, falling on his face, he will worship God, and report that God is in you of a truth." Now the false wares of the hypocrite appear naught, the mask is drawn off between God and their own consciences, Malachi iii. 1–3. But then the believer is found in Christ, for the word is never an enemy to the grace of the Spirit, "for he that doeth truth, cometh to the light, that his deeds may be made manifest, that they are wrought in God."

2. A time of temptation is a searching time. This is a sieve which Satan is allowed to manage for the discovery of the true grain. "Satan," said our Lord, to Peter, "hath desired to have you, that he might sift you as wheat." Sometimes Satan is, as it were, let loose, and temptations abound, iniquity is established by law, and then good and bad are put to the trial. Then the light corn and chaff appear, being driven away before the wind; the world begins to wonder after the beast, stars fall. Then goes the earthly, carnal-minded professor to the earth; the heady, unsettled, light professor, unstable as water, falls away; the proud, conceited professor appears as he is, like a tall barren tree. But then saints are found in Christ, sealed and safe; "for it is impossible to deceive the elect," Rev. vii. 1–3.

3. A season of the church's trouble, and of persecution for the gospel, is a searching time. A true friend is known in adversity. The stony ground receives the word and holds green, till the sun of persecution arise, and then it withereth. When Christ rides in triumph, many cry, Hosanna, who will afterwards cry, Crucify him. Many run after Christ in a day of peace, that will run as fast away from him in a day of trouble. This is God's sieve, with which he searcheth. They are brought to the waters of suffering, and then bowers down go away back. But the saints are now found in Christ, so that when "Israel is sifted as corn, not the least grain falls to the ground."

4. The time of death and judgment: this is the main thing, though not the only thing aimed at in the text. Possibly some may escape all the former searches, but none can escape this. Now the King indeed comes in to see the guests, and if there be but one hypocrite, he will instantly discover him. At present the corn and chaff are mixed, but then he will thoroughly purge his floor. Now foolish and wise virgins cannot easily be distinguished, but then it clearly appears who are wise and who are foolish. Now goats and sheep intermingle, but then they shall be for ever separated. Then the saints shall be found in Christ, and placed on his right hand. We now proceed,

II. To shew how and where they shall be found, that are found in Christ.

1. They shall be found in him, as branches in the true vine, John xv. 1–6. Being thus in him, they are in no hazard of the axe of God's wrath. Barren trees may, and shall be cut down for the fire; but Christ mystical is a tree which the axe may not, yea, cannot approach. "I the Lord do keep it; I will water it every moment lest any hurt it; I will keep it night and day." The pruning-knife, indeed, may come to it, to cut off the twigs of corruption; but this, instead of injuring, will render it

more fruitful. They are in no hazard of the wind, blow from what quarter it will. The wind of temptation and trouble may indeed shake, but cannot break nor remove the branches that are in Christ. They may be made by a violent blast to sweep the ground, but they will never be broken off.

2. They shall be found in a sanctuary, in a place of refuge. "The Lord shall be for a sanctuary to them." They have fled to him for refuge, and so shall find shelter in the worst of times. "Come, my people," says he, "enter thou into thy chambers, and shut thy doors about thee: hide thyself as it were for a little moment, until the indignation be overpast." When God came by a deluge to search the old world, he found them all eating and drinking; Noah only he found in the ark, and there he was safe. They who are in Christ, have laid hold on the horns of the altar: law and justice cannot drag them from it. They are within the city of refuge, where one drop of wrath cannot fall.

3. They shall be found under a covert, and in a hiding-place. The man Jesus shall be to them as an hiding-place from the wind, and a covert from the tempest. This is a covert of blood, the Mediator's blood, under which the guilty creature may sit safely, and abide the search of a holy God; for he sits there, clothed with an everlasting righteousnes, a white raiment, in which omniscience can see no spot. When God searcheth for the guilty creature, but finds him here, "then he is gracious to him, and saith, Deliver him from going down to the pit, I have found a ransom." There is blood sprinkled on the door-post where this man is, and therefore the destroying angel must pass by.

4. They shall be found in the covenant, in Christ's chariot, which is a safe place, Song iii. 9, 10; and so they shall be treated as God's own friends, even when he comes to render vengeance to his enemies, Isa. xxvii. 4, 5. We are now,

III. To give the reasons of the point.

1. God will search and find out every one of us, be where we will. "The King will come in to see the guests." We may sit at ease a while, but we must lay our account with a narrow search at last, which will try what metal we are of. There is no hiding from God. "Can any hide himself in secret places that I shall not see him? saith the Lord: Do not I fill heaven and earth? saith the Lord." Men may deceive themselves, and make a figure in their own eyes, when they are naught in the sight of the Lord. "But God is not, cannot be mocked." The world may be deceived, so that one limb of the devil may hate another, because he is so like a saint. The saints may be deceived, who may take them for full brethren, while they are not father's children. What if even hypocrites deceive the devil himself, in their religious fits, Jer. xvii. 9, 10; but God will find us out, "for he searcheth the reins and hearts, and will give unto every one according to his works."

2. If God find us, in this search, out of Christ, we are undone. We have nothing to shelter us, he will draw us out of our hiding-places and lurking holes; take off our mask, and spew us out of his mouth. We will be put away like dross, driven as the chaff before the wind, set among the goats, and separated for ever to destruction. "Neither is there salvation in any other: for there is none other name given under heaven among men, whereby we must be saved."

3. If we are found in Christ, we will be safe in time and eternity, blow the storm as it may. Temptations shall not totally carry us away, but we shall be born up against the stream. Troubles, though they get over our heads, yet we will find him "the lifter up of our heads," and we shall get safe on shore. When death comes, it shall be without its sting, seeing we are found in Christ; and at the day of judgment we shall be right hand men, because in him.

Use. Let it be your great care to be found in Christ. Our time is like to be a searching time of temptation and trouble; and though it should not, yet death and judgment are abiding us. What should we do to be carried through? Why, if you be found in Christ, as Noah in the ark, Lot in Zoar; you are in your chambers, "no evil shall befall you, nor plague come near your dwelling." Let not the searching time find you at a disadvantage; all those will be found so, who are in such a time,

1. Found in an unregenerate state, "dead in trespasses and sins, and without Christ." This is a dangerous and soul-ruining case to meet God in. God will find these men as Elijah found Ahab, "hast thou found me, O! mine enemy." Two cannot walk together except they be agreed; yet they may meet together, but surely there will be sad work when they meet. Dreadful will the meeting be, betwixt God and his enemies. When these meet, a consuming fire and dry stubble meet; a judge and a criminal. The Judge will say, "those mine enemies, which would not that I should reign over them, bring hither, and slay them before me."

2. Be not found with the sluggard, in your bed. Be not secure, as God found the old world. It is like that God will set fire into the nests of this generation, it were good to leave them in time, and shake off security; "to have our loins girt, and lamps burning." It was a sad case with Jonah, when he was drawn out of a sound sleep, and cast into a raging sea. It is awful to feel calamities, are we fear they are coming.

3. Be not found, as death finds the wicked, in the embraces of your lusts. "The wicked is driven away in his wickedness." The Philistines found Samson just risen out of Delilah's lap, without his hair. The soft embraces of our idols do but make way for severe strokes from the hand of God. It is difficult to conceive how a man may just make but a skip of it from the enjoyment of his lusts into Abraham's bosom. Nay, rather, God

will take these filthy garments, cover them with brimstone, and set them on fire about men's ears.

4. Be not found, like Saul, hid among the stuff. "Lay aside every weight, and the sin that doth most easily beset you." The world is like a long garment, which entangles a man, and unfits him to run and flee from the wrath to come. The rich man, who was thinking of nothing but full barns, and goods laid up for many years, was in a sad case when God found him out. Sit loose, then, to the world, if ever you would meet comfortably with God in the way of his judgments, here or hereafter.

Lastly, Be not found in the devil's camp, among ill company. "A companion of fools shall be destroyed." Lot's sons-in-law might have escaped, if they would but have left their ill company in Sodom, Gen. xix. 14, 15. Better go to the house of mourning, than to the house of feasting; the house of trembling, than of riot. "Blessed is the man that walketh not in the counsel of the ungodly, nor standeth in the way of sinners, nor sitteth in the seat of the scornful." But if you would abide the search here or hereafter, then be found in Christ.

1. Be found to be in him, united to him, by his Spirit and by faith. No storm can blow down those who are built upon this rock; neither will Christ lose a member of his body, in time or eternity. He is the true ark and refuge, "none perish that trust in him."

2. Be found walking in him. "As ye have therefore received Christ Jesus the Lord, so walk ye in him." Walking with him, before him, after his example, "walking even as he also walked." This is to walk in the way of holiness, "without which no man shall see the Lord."

Finally, Be found living in him, and upon him, Gal. ii. 20. Those that live in and by themselves will wither, when the trees planted in God's house will be flourishing.

MOTIVES, to urge you to make it your main business to be found in Christ, when God shall search for you in time and eternity:—

1. If you be found in Christ, he will be found in you, so shall you have a double security in a time of trial; for it is a mutual inbeing, John xvii. 21–23. He will be found in believers, as in his own house and lodging. Christ hath two lodgings: one in heaven. "He inhabiteth eternity, and dwells in the high and holy place." He hath another on earth, the believer's heart. "For he dwells with him also that is of a contrite and humble spirit." Christ hath bought both, and he made a journey to take possession of the house in heaven for us, Heb. vi. 20; and it is our own house, because it is his. "It is our house, which is from heaven." And he comes to the sinner's heart, to take possession of it for himself, and when they open to him by faith, he comes in and dwells, Rev. iii. 20. This will be a grand security. A man will always take care of his own house, especially in a storm, that the winds do not unroof it, or the rains waste it.

Christ will be found in you, as in his banqueting-house. The Pharisees wondered that he was a guest to sinners; and the world will not believe it, because they cannot see it. God's own children often say, how can these things be? Will he come into such a poor house to be entertained, where there is little or nothing with which to entertain him? They do not consider that Christ brings the provision with him. He is such a guest as Elijah was to the poor widow in a time of dearth, and feasts them in a time of the greatest trouble. "In the world," says he, "ye shall have tribulation; but be of good cheer, I have overcome the world; in me ye shall have peace."

He will be found in you, in his fortified house, as a conqueror. The first thing David did, after he received the kingdom, was to take the stronghold of Zion, which was so well fortified against him, that they thought the blind and the lame could hold it out, 2 Sam. v. 6, 7. So Christ, being anointed king, sets himself to recover the hearts of the elect, held out against him as a stronghold, by a blind understanding, and a lame and crooked will. "But he pulls down the strongholds, and casts down imaginations;" and having brought all to obedience, he comes in to hold it for himself. Now here is another security. Will he quit his conquest? No. "I give unto them" says he, "eternal life, and they shall never perish, neither shall any pluck them out of my hand."

4. His temple house, as the God of the temple. Believers are his temple; as the King of Glory, he hath come in, to dwell in their souls for ever. The soul that was a chapel for the devil, becomes the temple of Christ. There are sacrifices. They offer themselves to the Lord; their graces as incense, and he is the altar that sanctifies the gift. Another security; they shall be under special protection. "His eyes and his heart shall be on them perpetually." He will see to it, that the temple shall not be polluted; and though it should be laid in rubbish in a grave, it shall be gloriously rebuilt.

5. His garden. "I am come," says he, "into my garden, my sister, my spouse." They are a garden of spices, in which the precious plants of grace grow. This is another security. "He will water it every moment," hedge it about and preserve them, as a man doth his garden, while his other fields are exposed, Jer. xvii. 5, 6.

6. As a child in the mother's womb. "My little children," says Paul, "of whom I travail, as in birth again, until Christ be formed in you." "Christ is in them the hope of glory." This is another security. The mother cannot be executed in law, while she is with child, for that would be the death of two, whereas her life only is exposed.

Lastly, As the soul is in the body, Christ is their very life; he lives in them, Col. iii. 4; Gal. ii. 20; Acts ii. 25–27.

MOTIVE 2. If you be not found in Christ, you will be found in a bad case in time and eternity; in a trying time in this life, and in another world. You will be found as under the curse: laid open to the wrath of God, as the chaff to be driven away with the wind.

Sermon VIII.

*Not having mine own righteousness, which is of the
law, but that which is through the faith of Christ; the
righteousness which is of God, by faith.*

Philippians iii. 9.

In these words, the apostle describes the righteousness
in which he desires to be found and to compear[3] before
God, and this is the righteousness of Christ. It is not our
own, for to our own he opposeth it. It is not our faith,
for it is through and by faith. But it is the righteousness
of Christ, through the faith that hath him for its object.
The righteousness received by faith.

Doctrine. Christ's righteousness, received by faith,
is the sinner's only security to be depended upon before God. It is the sinner's only shield, shelter and defence, from the wrath of God. Here I shall,

I. Shew what is meant by Christ's righteousness.
II. How it is received by faith.
III. Confirm the doctrine. I am,
I. To shew what is meant by Christ's righteousness,
which is the sinner's only shield. Righteousness is the
result of obedience to the law. He who satisfies the law
is righteous, and this shelters from wrath. The great
thing that stands between God and a sinner is a broken
law; and while God is, it will be an effectual bar to keep
sinners out of heaven, to which the sinner can never

---

3   To appear in court before a judge.

come but with the good leave of the holy law, it being once satisfied. For this cause, seeing sinners could not satisfy the law for themselves, Christ undertook to do it for them. Accordingly, he fulfilled it, and by his fulfilling it, comes this righteousness which is the believer's security. Now Christ fulfilled the law in our room,

1. By his active obedience to its commands; perfect obedience to all the commands. This no mere man since the fall could do, yet it is that without which no man can be saved. It is a debt which must be paid for every one, either by themselves, or by their surety. The law saith to all the children of men, "If thou wilt enter into life, keep the commandments;" that is, keep them perfectly. Alas! then, must all perish? No. Christ answered for his own. What they could not do, he did. Now the law's demands of the sinner were very high.

DEMAND 1. Thy nature must be absolutely pure and spotless: for if the fountain be poisoned, how can the streams be wholesome. "Who can bring a clean thing out of an unclean? not one." Alas! the sinner can never answer this. He hath a corrupted nature, and he cannot purify it. "Who can say I have made my heart clean, I am pure from my sin." He was born in sin; he cannot get into his mother's belly, and be born over again without sin. Well, Christ satisfies this demand for his people, the law shall have all its asking; therefore the Son of God takes to himself a true body and a soul, both sinless. The ancient of days becomes an infant of days; he is conceived without spot, by the power of the Holy Ghost, and in due time born without sin. For as he was in his life, so was he in his birth, "holy, harmless, undefiled, and separated from sinners." His nature was not in the least tainted, but absolutely free of the least seed of sin. Here is now such a birth, such a nature as the law sought, so that demand is answered, that bar in the sinner's way is taken out; but the law has other demands.

Demand 2. Thou must give obedience to every command. Thy obedience must be as broad as the law. One hair's breadth lacking, thou shalt never see heaven. "Cursed is every one that continueth not in all things which are written in the book of the law, to do them." Alas! what shall the sinner do with this; there are many of these commands which he doth not know, how shall he obey them. Many quite against his nature, as "love your enemies." Many that, were his life a thousand times lying on them, and he would set himself to the utmost watchfulness, he will often break; such as vain thoughts, and impure desires.

Christ hath answered this demand. "He fulfilled all righteousness." "He did no sin, neither was guile found in his month." He made the law, he could not then but know every part of it; and he fulfilled it in every iota. He gave external and internal obedience; obedience in heart and life. Its hardest commands he opposed not; loved his enemies and denied himself; not a vain word ever dropt from his mouth, nor a vain thought ever entered his heart.

Demand 3. Every part of thy obedience must be raised up to the highest degree and pitch the law requires. "Thou shalt love the Lord thy God, with all thy heart, and with all thy soul, and with all thy mind." It is not enough that thou be sincere, and desire to do better, and be sorry thou canst not. Alas! the sinner can never answer this, he shall as soon reach the clouds. Let him do his best, corruption holds him down, so as he can never reach the top. If he be praying ever so fervently, there is always some coldrifeness in the heart. In his purest intentions, self-will insinuates itself.

Christ answered this demand. His love to his Father was more than seraphic. It was most ardent love. His love to men was incomparable, and went to the utmost bound of love. "For greater love hath no man than this, that a man lay down his life for his friends; but he laid down his life for his enemies." Every one of his actions was absolutely spotless and perfectly refined, without the least mixture of imperfection.

DEMAND 4. All this must be continued to the end, without the least failure in one iota, Gal. iii. 10. If thou shouldest all thy days live sinless, and at the hour of death a vain thought run through thy mind, all is gone. Alas! how impossible is this! The sinner cannot keep perfectly right one year, day, hour, minute, if a thousand hells were in it.

But Christ satisfied this demand. "He became obedient unto death, even the death of the cross." The first Adam made a fair outset, but he soon halted. The second continued to the end. The law could never catch him in the least sin from his cradle to his grave, by day or night, alone or in company. His heart and life shone in holiness in its meridian brightness, without the least cloud or spot, while his day lasted. So all these bars are removed by his active obedience. He fulfilled the law also,

2. By his passive obedience. When all these demands are answered, the law has another word with the sinner, ere he can enter within the gates of the city, and that is, taking sure hold of him, it says, "Pay what thou owest." Thou art in debt to the justice of God, for the sins already committed. Thou must satisfy the threatenings of the law, and bear the curse and vengeance thyself, or find a surety. O! then, "will the Lord be pleased with thousands of rams, or with ten thousands of rivers of oil? Shall I give my firstborn for my transgression, the fruit of my body for the sin of my soul?" No. These are all too mean to satisfy here. But, O! ye crowned heads, and mighty monarchs of the world, may not you be cautioners for the debt? No, they cannot, if they would sell their crowns, kingdoms, and dig up all the gold in the world, and lay it down, it would not pay their own debt; but they themselves must have

a cautioner, or they are ruined. O ye mighty angels! may not you rather undertake for this debt, than that your fellow-creatures should perish? They cannot. They are not able. They would be bankrupt with the payment of the thousandth part, and ruined for ever; and it would never be paid for them. O high demands indeed! that no creature in heaven or earth can answer. Then said the Mediator, "Lo, I come," Psal. xl. 7. What are thy demands?

Demand 1. Sinner, thou must suffer, thou must die the death, for the word is gone out of the Lord's month, "in the day thou eatest thereof thou shalt surely die." Alas! how shall this be answered? For if the sinner's life go for it, what hath he more? And if death once get him down, it will hold him down for ever. O! may not bearing crosses do it? No, the law must be satisfied with bearing curses, not crosses. O! may not tears for sin, bitter mourning, do it? No, it is shedding of blood, not pouring out of water, that the law must have. Without this, no remission of sin. But Christ satisfies this demand. It shall have all its asking. He puts himself to the sword of justice. Armed death falls upon him, sheds his precious blood, wounds him to the heart, separates soul and body, carries him away prisoner to the grave, and he is laid in the dust of death. Death gave him the first fall, but because he was God, he riseth again; and death having got his due, he brings away the keys of hell and death with him, that never one of his may be prisoner there.

Demand 2. Thy sufferings must be universal in the whole man, for so hath thy sinning been. That body of thine, the instrument of sin, must suffer. That head, that hath contrived so much mischief, must be wounded; that heart, that has been the spring of all, must be pierced; these feet, which have carried thee so often to sin, and these hands, that have wrought so much iniquity, must also be pierced. And that soul of thine must also suffer principally, us being the chief actor of all thou hast done against God. Ah! how shall we bear it? Who can endure this, which is a thousand deaths in one? Christ satisfies this demand also. He suffers in his body. His head was crowned and pierced with thorns. "His heart was melted like wax in the midst of his bowels." "His feet and hands were pierced." "His tongue did cleave to his jaws." "His bones were all out of joint." His body had nothing to cover it but shame, and his strength was dried up like a potsherd. The wrath of God fell on his soul. It was troubled, sore amazed, and agonized. The arrows dipped in the curse were shot against it, till the law had no more to require.

DEMAND 3. Thy sufferings must be most exquisite; thou shalt have no pity, no sparing, but judgment without mercy, Deut. xxix. 20. Ah! who can satisfy this? "Who can dwell with devouring fire?" "It is a fearful thing to fall into the hands of the living God." Christ satisfies this too. "God spares him not, but delivers him up to the death for us all." Though his body was of a most refined temperature, and so his senses most exquisite, his death was of the most tormenting kind. His eyes were denied the light of the sun, his ears heard their cruel mockings, and he got vinegar to drink. He was in travailing pangs, and soul travail. No help had he in it. Men nor angels did not help him, and he died in it.

DEMAND 4. Thy sufferings must be infinite, for it is infinite justice that thou hast offended. Ah! who can bear this? This is killing; saddest of all, a thousand times. Universal, exquisite; yet infinite, ever to endure, never to end. "Who can abide with everlasting burnings?" This is the hell of hells, and beyond the reach of a creature, a finite being. But Christ answers this too. He is God, therefore an infinite one; so his sufferings, though not infinite in duration, yet infinite in value, fully answering the demands of the law.

Last DEMAND. Thy sufferings must be voluntary, for God hates robbery for burnt-offering. If thou murmur in the least, under all thy sufferings, it is new sin; a blemish in the sacrifice, which prevents its acceptance. Ah! who can do this? The weight of wrath makes the devils and the damned roar against God. A man can scarcely bear a fit of the gout or gravel, or even a sharp pain of any kind, but with some impatience. But Christ satisfies this too. "When he was oppressed and afflicted, he opened not his mouth." In all his sufferings, he never had the least wrong thought of God rising in his heart, Psal. xxii. 1–3. Never the least murmuring or fretting. He willingly underwent what he was to suffer. He did not flee when his hour came. He prayed for his enemies, his murderers, in the very extremity of his sufferings, in a meek and loving manner, saying, "Father, forgive them, for they know not what they do." Let us,

II. Shew how this righteousness is received by faith. It is received and becomes ours by faith, as faith unites us to Christ. Upon this union, follows a communion with Christ in his righteousness; so Christ being ours by faith, his righteousness is ours. The soul, by faith, marries with Christ, and the righteousness is its dowry. The soul flies to Christ as the city of refuge, and that righteousness is their cover. We now proceed,

III. To confirm the doctrine.

1. That only can shelter us from the wrath of God which satisfies his law. Now this righteousness is the only thing which can satisfy his law, and it has done it fully. The law is magnified more by his obedience and sufferings than if all the elect had gone to hell for it. The law being obeyed, and executed upon Christ, is more magnified than it could have been by them, and that because of the dignity of the person. Even as a king shews a greater respect to the law, by executing it on his own son, than upon a thousand common malefactors. They would have been ever satisfying, but never could have

fully satisfied. By Christ it gets both active and passive obedience, by them only passive.

2. It is the righteousness of God. It is so called, because it is the righteousness of him who is God, Jer. xxiii. 6; therefore it is called, gold tried in the fire. Our gold is become dross, it will not abide the touchstone of the law, because imperfect, but Christ's righteousness will. Ours will not abide the fire of the judgment of the God of truth. Our obedience is not full measure, and, being weighed in the balance of the sanctuary, it will be found light.

It is the only righteousness accepted of God. "In whom," says he, "I am well pleased." It may be safely depended upon, for it is of infinite value. "Christ purchased the church with his own blood." It was the divine nature of Christ that made all his obedience so efficacious for the benefit of his people. What sins will not the blood of the Son of God purge away? "It cleanseth from all sin."

3. It is the righteousness contrived by the only wise God to save sinners, when nothing else could do it, Psal. xl. 6, 7. When there was no help among angels or men for them, he laid help on the Mediator, as one mighty to save. This was a contrivance becoming an infinite God. The mercy of God shines forth in it, finding an object in the deepest misery. To have given a deliverance from wrath, after millions of years, would have been great mercy; but here is mercy, bringing the sinner from the lowest abyss of misery unto the highest pitch of happiness. Here, also, the justice of God shone gloriously. In the deluge, and the burning of Sodom, it appeared, but more here. It got all its demands. What are all creatures, to the Son of God suffering? The love of God was displayed. "God so loved the world, that he gave his only begotten Son." The Son willingly gave himself. Here is love, wonderful indeed in all its dimensions. Behold also the wisdom of God. The confused mass at the be-

ginning was not comparable to the confusion at the fall. But truth met with mercy. Out of the sin that obscured the glory of God, is brought the greatest honour. The matter is so ordered, that man stands more firmly than under the first covenant. When the angels stood astonished, hell rejoiced at the fall. Man lay grovelling in the dust of misery, wisdom found out a way for restoring them to happiness.

USE 1. Never entertain low thoughts of sin. It is the worst of evils, which could not be remedied, but by the sufferings of Christ. It brings a heavy burden on a sinner that bears his own burdens. Behold it in the glass of Christ's sufferings, and you will think none of it little. Sin runs counter to the nature of God, and dishonours all his attributes. God is the chief good, sin the worst evil. The sinner dares God's justice, presumes on his mercy, mocks his patience, challengeth his power, despiseth his love, and invades his sovereignity. So Christ behoved to suffer the most extreme punishment, to honour his justice and glorify all his perfections.

Sin contradicts his will. The foolish contradicts the laws of infinite wisdom, casts off God's laws and make its own lusts laws, and, therefore, to blot out this dishonour, the Son is made a sacrifice.

When God had perfected the frame of the world, and it remained only that he should have his tribute of glory paid to him out of it, sin gave a rude shock to the whole work, shook the whole frame; therefore was there such dreadful work to repair it, the Mediator suffering, rocks rending, the sun not shining, &c.

USE 2. Never entertain low thoughts of pardon. Every pardon is the price of blood, more precious than a thousand worlds. Pardoning sin is one of the greatest letters of God's name, one of the greatest of his works, greater than to make a world. When God said, let such a thing be, it was. But when sin is to be pardoned, justice stands up for satisfaction; the truth of God for the honour of a broken law. Wisdom is set to work to find out a way, the Son pays down the price of his blood, Num. xiv. 17–19.

Use 3. Come to Christ for shelter under his righteousness, that you may be justified, pardoned, and accepted. Consider there is no other way but this to the divine favour, no shelter from the sting of unpardoned guilt but here. All other will be but fig-leaf covers.

Is not pardon of sin, and acceptance with God, worth the seeking? It makes a man happy, Psal. xxxii. 1. A man may be rich and yet reprobate, great in this world and yet damned in the next. His portion fat, yet his soul lean. But a justified man is a happy man. Worldly things come from God's hand, but this great blessing from his heart. It will be sweet sauce to the bitterest dish; it will cause you to glory even in tribulation. The righteousness of Christ justifies a man, and this makes every bitter water sweet. "For there is no condemnation to them that are in Christ Jesus. It is God that justifieth, who is he that condemneth?"

And if you would give evidence of your interest in imputed righteousness, you must do it by inherent righteousness. Shew your faith by your works. Faith without works is dead, being alone. Amen.